Peace in My Time?!

One Scouser's War

Peace in My Time?!

One Scouser's War

JOHN WOODS

Palatine Books, 1995

for Michael and Katherine

Peace in My Time: One Scouser's War
Copyright © John Woods, 1995

Published by Palatine Books, an imprint of Carnegie Publishing Ltd, Preston
Typeset in 10½ / 12 Ehrhardt by Carnegie Publishing Ltd
Printed by T. Snape & Co., Preston

British Library Cataloguing-in-Publication Data
A CIP catalogue record for this book is available from the British Library

ISBN 1-874181-11-X

Farewell Scottie Road!

IN the spring of 1942 I had temporarily left Scotland Road for all points south following a stupid family row with my father. Like most Scousers I found it difficult to settle and yearned for home but was determined not to return with my tail between my legs. So, in a fit of youthful bravado and jingoistic naivety, I had a few pints, went into a recruiting office in Ipswich, lied about my age and signed up for King and Country. Feeling quite the man, I returned home and had my dignity reinstated by a warm family welcome. Thus I awaited the call.

The fateful day finally arrived, 6 May 1942. I woke up early at 6.30 a.m., although my train was not until 9.40. I hoped to avoid upsetting, embarrassing farewells but, on coming downstairs, there sat my Mam and Dad. She, despite the façade of Scottie Road toughness, looked very distressed; she had obviously been crying, complete with red nose and eyes. Forgetting my teenage machismo, I filled up and did everything I could to hide my emotions; father, like most working-class men, did the same.

'Oh, have a cup of tea and some toast,' Mam said, breaking the strained silence.

'That'll be great,' I spluttered, anything to keep normal. My mother then appeared to erupt with emotion; semi-choked instructions poured forth with the tea, – to look after myself, to behave, not to act the clown and to keep out of fights. I tried to reply with the usual cheek that I would be fine, having trained for over sixteen years on Scotland Road and so the army could offer few surprises. Mam looked as though she would clout me.

'He's right, Mary Ellen, he's right!' Dad rose with a chuckle. He then brought out his own small leather case for my few possessions and gave me some sandwiches for the journey.

'I'll come with yer to Lime Street,' he offered.

'No Dad, I'll be fine. You get to work,' I refused, as quickly and diplomatically as possible; I did not want to hurt his feelings but felt a Lime Street station goodbye scene would prove too much.

'Better be goin', don't want to wake up the kids.' I picked up the case, glancing upstairs where my younger brothers slept on.

'Bit early yet, lad,' Dad said, as Mam began to cry.

'Look after yerselves, better go, God bless!' I beat my first hasty but dignified retreat down the lobby and out into Olivia Street. Dad followed and shook hands as tears welled up all round. 'Good luck, son.'

I literally ran down the street and along Stanley Road. It was great to be out in the fresh air. I strolled purposefully along Scottie Road, Taylor Street and down to Great Homer Street. I had to pay a visit to old 'Bosi', where memories of childhood whispered from the flags. I looked up at the 'mission hall,' the hollow, Jack Parry's stable and our old house, number twenty-two. Then one of the old neighbours, Lizzie Rankins, who lived opposite, shouted the morning greeting and asked where I was off. 'On me way to the army,' I shouted.

'Go away, yer not old enough,' she replied.

'Lied about me age.'

'Oh.' She said nonplussed. 'Remember me to yer Mam!' A strange instruction given what I had just said.

I went up to the top of 'Bosi', along Scottie Road and loitered outside St Anthony's Church. It must have been the emotion of it all, but I experienced an uncharacteristically religious urge to go in. There, with the solitude of the pews contrasting with the bustle outside, I prayed earnestly to keep the family safe till I got home. I never considered the possibility that I would not return.

Thus, confident of my own immortality, I then caught the number twenty-four tram to the station where hundreds of servicemen milled around. All seemed in better spirits than me. After a few inquiries I found a seat by a window in an otherwise full compartment. The train filled rapidly, corridors packed with people and cases. In childhood I had considered our house overcrowded, but it could not beat this. With the usual series of jolts and splutters, we pulled out of Lime Street. Almost immediately everyone in the compartment began to read their papers and I pulled out the 'Daily Mirror'. The Liverpool sky had been dull and overcast but once out in the countryside it started raining 'cats and dogs'. Rain poured down the window, reflecting my private gloom. Then a pleasant older man opposite offered me his 'Reader's Digest'. Half an hour passed and to break the monotony I decided to go to the toilet, squeezing along the corridor. On my return I found my seat occupied by a big fellow in an RAF uniform.

'That's my seat!' I said, attempting to sound authoritative.

'You sure?' He growled.

'Dead sure. There's me case on the rack and that 'Reader's Digest' you've got belongs to this gentleman,' I answered, aggressively grabbing at the book. After a few seconds of 'staring each other out' he rose and returned to the corridor, obviously discussing my brass nerve with his mates.

'Good for you; he thought you were a kid going back to school,' said my fellow passenger.

'Me, what! I'm off to the army!' I replied with bruised dignity. 'Oh,' he laughed, 'I've been visiting Liverpool for a couple of days, bit of business. Now back to Watford—retired customs officer, me. Fancy a cigarette?' I refused but went on to have a long chat before he decided to go to the toilet.

'Would you like any help?' I offered.

'Certainly not!' he replied indignantly. On his return he had obviously had a word with my buddies in the RAF and assured me that there would be no problems at Euston.

Eventually we arrived; I bade the guy farewell and was then swept along in a sea of chaos to Waterloo Station which itself looked like a cattle stampede. With no time for the sights, I jumped on the train to Norwich and the barracks. It proved to be yet another crowded compartment full of fellows carrying small cases, all joining up. Curiously no one spoke; I must admit I was a bit relieved as, with my accent, I doubt if I would have been intelligible. Finally in Norwich I was directed towards an army truck with the other new arrivals; already Scotland Road seemed a lifetime away ...

2

You're in the army now!

I T WAS DIFFICULT to see out of the crowded truck on our journey to the barracks but the countryside looked pleasant enough despite the rain. The truck stopped and we were ordered in true army spirit to dismount. Therein followed our first taste of army lecturing; we were told we were now soldiers but would receive proper training before we would be of any use to the war effort. All this was delivered with the usual threatening, semi-sadistic overtones. We were then bundled off to the office block for our first taste of army red tape. I glanced around, noting the huge size of the barracks, about four storeys high. There were other buildings attached to the main one forming three sides of a square, the centre of which was to become the dearly-beloved parade ground. Soldiers were already drilling and the whole place echoed with the yell of orders. I was relieved to reach the office for some peace and quiet.

Quickly our names were called and we went in turn to a counter and were ordered to stand upright as we gave the necessary particulars. Then a soldier with two stripes roared for silence. You could have heard a pin drop.

'When you hear your name called, move to that counter fast. You can run if you like, but no more ambling. The bloody war will be over before you lot get your number!'

Then the famous number, the one you learned and remembered for the rest of your life. Then again we were yelled at to get outside and were quickly sorted into groups to be taken to our sleeping quarters. It was only 2.30 p.m. but I felt a lot of us had already had enough.

NCOs then took us to what had once been the stables; the original cobble stones were visible on the floor. Down each side there were two-tier bunks and in the centre a table and cast-iron stove. The corporal in charge allocated the bunks and the adjacent steel lockers for our kit. Then off again to collect blankets, straw pillow and three small mattresses. After sorting out the bedding, we were then issued with uniforms, boots, shirts, socks *et al.* Then the corporal produced two hammers and some steel punches impressed with numbers from zero to nine. He explained as aggressively as possible, as was the army way, that these were to be used to punch our army number into our boots. For the same purpose he produced a stencilling set to be used on all our clothes. The big laugh was that most of us looked dumbfounded; we could not re-member the damned number without looking at our AB64, our now seemingly essential identity card.

Before we could start we were told to hurry to the cookhouse for high tea in the British army. The cookhouse was massive, an extension to the main barracks. We all collected a big white mug each and made our way in an orderly queue to a long steel counter laden with buckets full of tea. We filled our own mugs and then the lads were moaning like mad, refusing the cake and sniffing at the tea with disgust. All I could imagine was that they had never 'roughed it' before. We had to swill our mugs clean and return them to the counter. Later we were issued with our own enamel mugs.

On our return to the stable the corporal in charge, a nasty piece of work, told us we had to have all our belongings numbered by 'lights out' at eleven. He was an obvious barrack room soldier, instantly surveying us and choosing his victims in order to bolster his authority. He seemed to bark perma-nently.

'You call me "corporal" each time you speak to me!' seemed to ring incessantly around the stable. God knows what he would have been like with any proper rank. He yelled again to begin the numbering as chaos erupted. Over thirty men grappled for the equipment. It was at this point I made my first friend; the guy in the bunk above leaned down.

'Don't bother dashing around like the rest of the idiots. Just give them an hour or so and then we'll have no trouble getting our stuff marked.' He then introduced himself as John Peel, a Londoner. Before I could answer he said, 'You're scouse.' It seems odd looking back, but that was the first time I had been called 'scouse'. I laughed at this name; I thought I'd heard the lot on 'Scottie'.

'Who are you bluffin'?' Nevertheless he insisted on the name. To me he seemed an old man, at least twenty-seven. Most of us in the stable were in our teens, some, like myself, having lied about their 'age. While the others darted around for tools we chatted, only to be rudely interrupted by our bellowing corporal. He yelled as to why we were not marking our kit; Peel replied cooly that we had until eleven. I tried unsuccessfully to suppress a smirk but it was too late, the damage was done. The corporal went berserk, screeching mainly at me.

'I give the orders here! Start marking that kit!' I gave the same reply as Peel. I later realised that I had been chosen as the fall-guy in this bloke's attempt to impose his authority. Peel was too old and streetwise.

'Try to get a hammer from one of the others,' Peel instructed in a terse voice. As I obeyed the corporal again went into a fit of shouting.

In aggressive exasperation I shouted, 'You get the hammer for me if you like! Or shut yer gob before I do it for yer!'

Peel jumped off the bunk in an effort to stop the inevitable.

'If this goes any further will you report it?' The stable was silent.

'No I won't,' replied the corporal slowly, and quite deliberately he threw a punch at me. We both got stuck in; it only lasted a couple of minutes, leaving me none the worse for the scrap, but the NCO finished up with a black eye, split lip and a badly bruised hand, I could not claim the credit for the latter as he hit one of the bunks by mistake. He left quickly and the barracks returned to normal.

Peel and I got all our marking done well before eleven but he warned me to be very careful as the corporal would have mates who would be determined to keep a raw recruit in his place.

The next morning we had to parade in our uniforms and collect our rifles. Peel had spotted the corporal talking to the sergeant in charge of us. 'Whatever happens on parade, don't answer either of them back under any circumstances,' he hissed.

I behaved, but the sergeant was nevertheless quick to inform me that I was on a charge (252) for striking an NCO. All the lads agreed it was a dirty trick; the corporal had inadvertently developed an *esprit de corps* among us. The sergeant himself had not inspired respect, a typical old regular who had served for years in India and was brought back to England to train us 'civvies'. He was good at giving orders but I would have wished him to hell in real combat. I honestly think it was his type and officers of a similar mentality which lost Britain the initiative at the beginning of the war. They were all too busy reading the rule book.

Thus on my third day in the army my name and number were publicly displayed on a board in the stable simply stating 'CO's orders'. I referred to Peel for elaboration. He said I would have to see the captain, but I was still not prepared for what followed. At 2.00 p.m. the sergeant and two soldiers marched me into the CO's office, accompanied by the usual 'Hat off, left, right, left, right *et al.* It all seemed like an old Frank Randle movie. There behind a desk sat the captain, yet another ex-India regular who had worked his way up through the ranks; God knows how. I just assumed it was because he had the loudest voice.

The sergeant screeched out the charge. The captain became absorbed in a list of rules and regulations and enthusiastic eulogies about order and discipline. He then asked me if I had anything to say for myself.

'I joined up, sir, to fight the Germans, not the English. Still, I'm sorry for what happened,' I added on Peel's advice. The captain looked sceptical.

'I award you fourteen days' CB.' So, confined to barracks was my punishment. The sergeant started yelping again. I got the impression that I was to report to the guardroom every night, from whence I was directed to the cookhouse and a mass of greasy dishes. Another chap and I were to amuse ourselves washing them. I can't even remember his crime. Thus began one auspicious army career. I had the funny feeling that things were not going to improve.

3

We'll make a man of you yet!

DURING the next six weeks of training, life certainly had its ups and downs. The cookhouse where I did my CB consisted of a plethora of ovens and sinks regularly stacked high with a multitude of dirty dishes, all oozing grease. Unlike home, to be fair, there was plenty of washing up liquid and boiling hot water. The cooks turned out to be a decent crowd, regularly giving me and my fellow offender soup, toast, bacon, the odd egg and gallons of strong tea. Thus, I would have quite happily stayed there, although it was exhausting after a day's training.

The first weeks of training were the worst of my army career. Although réveillé was not until 7.00 a.m., most of the lads got up earlier to wash and shave. The facilities provided for our ablutions were pre-historic, never mind pre-war. They appeared to be wooden horse troughs which went right around the walls at a height of 2′ 6″. Similarly down the middle of the room, two more lines of troughs had been installed. All were serviced by about seventy or so taps about a yard apart. They were supposed to cater for over two hundred men, hence washing became synonymous with bedlam. I was lucky in that I still did not have to shave at the time but when our sergeant found out that a few of us enjoyed this perk, he ordered that all would have to shave, a procedure he would supervise. I thought this, like a good many other rules in the army, was a load of old cobblers and took delight in getting round it by lathering my face and removing the soap with a razor minus blade. Nevertheless, the sergeant looked pleased.

After this we soon fell into a routine of duties, stripping down our beds, neatly folding our blankets and generally tidying up the stable before donning our PT shorts, vests and pumps. To be fair, this emphasis on a routine involving 'mucking in', cleanliness and tidiness probably helped to preserve harmony in some post-war marriages.

We had to be on parade at 7.30 a.m. sharp with the PT corporal. Breakfast was served between 8.00 a.m. and 8.30 a.m. and for the first few days we paraded again at 9.00 a.m. There were also various visits to the doctor, dentist and barber and not least the tailor's shop for uniform alterations. We spent time learning how to march, run and handle rifles. Later we went through the usual target practice with other weapons like the sten and bren guns and the 2 " mortar.

Then came the route marches dreaded by some. The distance involved was regularly increased, as was the equipment we had to carry, until we could cope with a run of twenty miles. This, then, became a fixed length. Once we had mastered this to our betters' satisfaction, forced marches were arranged between rival squads, as were gruelling cross-country runs. Some poor chaps suffered with terrible blisters on their feet courtesy of the training and the heavy army boots. Yet we all stoically accepted our lot. On the Friday of the first week we finally had our injections catering for any posting and were then told we were all excused duties for forty-eight hours until Monday morning. To most it seemed like a gift from the gods, the army with a human face, but in reality it was a crafty ploy, boosting morale and, more importantly, allowing quite a few raw recruits to get over the swollen arms and nausea the needles had bestowed.

On a personal note, my 'discourtesy' to the corporal had not been forgotten, as others took on his vendetta. The morning after I had visited the CO's office, a PT corporal in black track suit embellished with crossed swords on the arms, strutted

past and, glaring straight into my eye, muttered vehemently
'You Scouse bastard!' I held my tongue, remembering Peel's
advice. He continued this ritual humiliation for the rest of the
week. He seemed to personify all the PT instructors I was to
meet in the services, peacocks loving to flaunt their muscular
dexterity, screeching in high-pitched voices as though something
was gripping their private parts, and yet surprisingly doing little
in the way of real combat. By Friday enough was enough. I could
control my temper no longer. To give in to such treatment
flouted all the known rules of Scottie Road etiquette.

'You Scouse bastard,' he growled repetitively.

'Wanna prove that, mate?' I angrily retorted.

'Yeah. If you've got the guts, be in the gym at 12 o'clock
on Saturday and we'll settle this properly in the boxing ring.'

'Nothing, my dear sir, would give me greater pleasure,' I
replied, hamming a swashbuckling scene in a Hollywood film,
'but, unfortunately I have a prior engagement at the cookhouse.'

'Never mind that, I'll settle everything with your platoon
sergeant.'

'Done,' I answered cheerfully. In my naive brashness I was
'made up'. It had all gone on long enough and I longed to
teach the PT instructor his own personal lesson for picking
on some of the lads.

After injections on the Friday, Peel repeatedly told me to
cancel the fight. By the next day, he warned, I might be well
below par. 'No chance,' I replied, remembering the Liver-
pudlian rules of engagement, 'I'm going to give that bastard
a good hiding.'

'Ever heard of famous last words?' said Peel with the wisdom
of his twenty-seven years.

Saturday noon arrived. Like Gary Cooper I was in the gym,
which was packed with all our platoon, some PT corporals
and even the captain who had awarded me my CB. It was
going to be a major event. The captain was armed with a
stopwatch and bell, symbols of fair play. A PT corporal was
appointed as my second; there were to be three, three-minute

rounds. Excitedly the lads formed a square. The bell went. My God, I discovered right away that the fellow was no mug; this guy was a real fighter. Despite the cheering by the second round I was getting the hiding of my life and by a blurred third, I was wishing the floor would open up and swallow me. By now I could only see through one battered eye; the other had packed in. Somehow I managed to stay the distance, a 1940s Sylvester Stallone.

As I stumbled through the crowd, my PT second muttered, 'He took a liberty with you, kid.'

'Why?' I moaned.

'Well, lad, you've just fought the ex-middleweight champion of the British Isles.'

'I think every part of me is telling me that', I managed to grin ruefully, longing for my bunk.

Back at the barracks, some of the lads seemed disappointed and I felt I had let them down. Peel, on the other hand, was beside himself with rage. 'We'll have him for this! We'll have him for this!' he ranted repeatedly.

'I've already considered it, pal, but I think I'll forget it. I'm just not good enough,' I replied wearily. Peel persisted and then disappeared for a couple of hours, peace at last to lick my wounds. Later that afternoon he told me excitedly that he had discovered where the PT guy drank in town. 'We'll have him when he comes out of the pub tonight,' He muttered ominously.

'Oh, on yer way!' I said. 'Don't yer think we should wait a while? Look at me face, not exactly inconspicuous. Besides, I'm achin' all over.'

Peel would not have it, so against my marginally better judgement we got ready and, breaking God knows how many rules in the book, set off for a pub in Norwich. The place was packed with servicemen of all types and nationalities plus the usual bevy of local girls having what would turn out to be the time of their lives. It was about 9.00 p.m. We squeezed our way through the throng and espied the PT corporal at a table

with a sergeant and a couple of girls. They spotted us immediately. My heart sank as the instructor grinned malevolently
Peel piped up. 'Well, there's nothing for it. I'll take the sergeant, you go for the PT guy. Make it quick and we'll get out
fast.' All hell seemed to erupt. I vaguely remember reaching
for a bottle and hitting a head as the corporal lunged at me.
He seemed to drop to the floor. Peel had seen off the sergeant
and speedily dragged me from the pub. 'Come on, let's jump
a train to London,' he shouted hurriedly. 'I've a few good
mates down there.'

'What, desert? You're crazy!' I panted. God only knew what
fate awaited me after this latest stunt, but desertion seemed
dangerously over the top, even for me. A lengthy discussion
ensued, the closest Peel and I came to an argument, but I
refused to go to London and he eventually agreed to return
to the barracks. The significance of the evening's events and
suggestions would only become apparent later in the friendship.
I was just relieved at this point to be back at the barracks
before 'lights out' at 11 p.m.

Anticipating further trouble back in our stable, Peel asked
a couple of lads to change bunks with us. We all waited. Just
after 1 a.m. the stable door opened and moonlights streamed
into the room. I counted fifteen heads coming in quietly. One
of the intruders switched on a torch and shone it on to my
usual bunk. Realising it was not me, one of them shouted,
'Okay, where's the Scouser?' Silence. Genuinely frightened, I
grabbed hold of my steel helmet, intent on smashing it on
anyone who came too close. Some of the gang proceeded to
work their way down the room again asking for me. As they
approached, suddenly the main light came on and there stood
Peel, looking a little ridiculous in just his shirt, but waving a
.303 rifle like a baseball bat.

'If any of you touches Scouse, I'll break a few heads before
you get out,' he said with real menace.

'Don't worry lad, we just want a chat,' replied the PT corporal,
noticeable for the very large plaster across his forehead.

'Only takes one to chat,' Peel retorted emphatically.

'Fair enough, all of you go outside, but wait for me,' the PT guy instructed his pals.

'John, do you want to talk to this bloke?' Peel shouted.

Still gripping the helmet tightly, I muttered, 'Let him speak from where he is!'

To my astonishment the NCO replied, 'Okay, pal, let's call it quits and shake on it.'

'Sure but let's leave it till the morning, sort it out then,' I said warily.

'Right, twelve o'clock tomorrow.' With that the corporal left as I viewed the next day with some trepidation. After all that had happened, my distrust verged on paranoia. Sunday arrived and at 11.30 a.m. the PT instructor came to our stable, his forehead still painfully swollen and Peel suggested that the two of us went off for a chat. Off we went and as we got near the NAAFI the corporal invited me into the NCO canteen for a cup of tea.

'No way, it's against the rules,' I said.

'Leave that to me, most of the others will be in the dining hall having their Sunday lunch or still in bed,' he replied reassuringly. So in we went, he purchasing some tea and several aptly named rock cakes. As we sat down, a couple of NCOs approached to join us. 'Private chat, lads,' the corporal said as they took the hint and went out to sit elsewhere.

'Well, I'll say one thing for you, kid, you've got bottle,' he smiled as he touched the plaster on his forehead. 'You could be a good little boxer with some training—too much enthusiasm and not enough technique at the moment,' he added with a professional air.

'Well, you should know, yer knocked the shit out of me,' I replied slowly but surely relaxing. He then asked where I had learned to fight and we swapped boxing stories. I unwound and with steady confidence I could even make him laugh. He then said I would not have to finish my CB: it had, after all, been somewhat unfair. He told me just to report to the regimental police in the guardroom and he would see to the rest. ''Cuse me, are you Scouse?' The shrill voice of the waitress interrupted the conversation.

'Yeah, why?' I replied.

'There's a fellow next door asking after you,' she said glancing towards the hatch door which divided the NCOs' facilities from those of the mere rookies. The corporal rose and opened it to find a concerned Peel furtively peering into the room.

'Your guardian angel's here,' the NCO laughed.

'Well, time to be off. Thanks for the tea.' In a gesture of mutual sincerity and respect, we shook hands warmly. Peel gaped in disbelief.

4

War Games

OVER the next few weeks old J. P. and I became good friends, pulling a few tricks together and certainly having our share of laughs. He told me that he has been brought up in Shoreditch and had had a fairly rough childhood. His father had disappeared when he was ten, leaving his mother to fend for herself with three children, Peel being the eldest. After that he remembered a succession of 'uncles'; eventually one stayed for good. J. P. was never sure if this bloke and his mum had bothered to marry but all he knew was that the new stepdad hated him and Peel reciprocated the feeling. Thus at fourteen he could take it no longer and upped and went to live with his grandmother. She died soon after and then he was forced to look after himself working in hotels, mainly in the West End. I told him a bit about Scottie Road and we seemed to have shared similar upbringings, making ends meet in a common experience of poverty.

Such stories were exchanged in-between our training. The forced marches continued, with battle training on special effects courses. Again we received repeated practice in weapon training including 2 " mortars, piats, sten guns, Thompson machine guns and the Bren gun, the latter being the most reliable and dependable weapon in the British army according to the bellowing instructors. Some of the lads complained that the training was too hard, but I could never understand what they were moaning about; after Scottie Road, it seemed a doddle. Still, training was not without its risks and one day J. P. and

I had a close call. We were training with 2″ mortars. There would always be two men involved in the routine. Number one would lie down holding the mortar barrel for direction while number two would lie alongside, unscrew a cap on the bomb to expose a copper top and then slide it into the barrel fins first. The bomb would fly out in seconds. On impact the copper top would produce the explosion. On this particular afternoon I was number one, Peel two. As we started, J. P. unscrewed the cap and slid the bomb into the barrel. In silent disbelief I noticed he had put in the copper top first. I brought the barrel down sideways as quickly as I could at the same time smacking J. P. in the face so that he would turn his head away. The corporal in charge was amazed. 'What the hell are you doing?'

'Saving his life! Stay where you are; the copper top's gone in first!' I yelled. Luckily the bomb did not strike the bottom of the barrel. I gingerly slid the bomb out, quickly replacing the cap for safe keeping. I looked around and saw old J. P. was as white as a sheet while the training corporal was speechless.

J. P. was always asking me to go to the 'Smoke' with him on leave. He promised to show me around London, pointing out that it was all but impossible for me to get home to Liverpool on a forty-eight hour pass. In any case I just could not afford it. I was getting three shillings (15p) a day when I joined up but after sending some home to my mother I used to finish up with ten shillings and ninepence (53p) a week. Out of this came all the sundries like NAAFI rations, soap and later razor blades. Despite my lack of 'readies,' J. P. kept on insisting I go to London with him and saying he would cover the costs. After days of nagging I eventually agreed but did not like the idea of 'bumming' from him. We got off at Waterloo and met up with two mates of his accompanied by two girls. God knows how, but they must have known we were coming. My first impression was instant classification, two 'spivs' and two prostitutes. We then proceeded to a huge pub, which like every other, was packed with service personnel.

I was introduced to a whole gang of people and then the manageress who seemed to be a very close friend, showed us our room. A slap up meal followed and then out for a walk around the local sights. It was then I heard one friend pass an odd comment about J. P. being back in the army again. Peel quickly 'snuffed' this conversation and I was having too marvellous a time to press the subject.

The leave flew by and too soon it was time to head back to the barracks. I noticed on our way to the train that Peel was wearing a very heavy plated gold ring; it looked really impressive. 'Where did yer get that?' I gawped.

'Oh, one of the girls picked it up somewhere. Gave it to me—she's a bit soft on me,' he replied as we made our return to normality.

About a week later, with training drawing to a close, J. P. suggested a few pints in town. Money, as ever, was tight so I agreed but insisted I would just have a couple. 'Some good old civvie might treat us,' retorted J. P. Civilians buying service personnel the odd pint was still a reasonably common gesture at this point in the war but that particular night we were out of luck and both down to our last coppers. I noticed J. P. had begun to play very conspicuously with the gold ring. He then asked to see the manager and proceeded to negotiate a loan of £5 till Monday using the ring as security. 'Expecting a postal order from my mother,' he explained to a somewhat sceptical publican. It was 9.30 p.m. and half an hour of drinking time left. At first the guy seemed uninterested; Peel then asked for £6 and said if he failed to show on Monday, the bloke could keep the ring. J. P. encouraged the bloke to have a good look at it; it was 22 ct. gold and very heavy. It is by now a fact of life that some pub managers made a fortune in these garrison towns during the war buying jewellery *et al.* from troops desperate for ready cash and another pint. The guy looked suitably impressed and gave J. P. a fiver and two ten shilling notes. As soon as he had left the table J. P. snapped, 'Drink up! Come on, come on!'

'But it's only quarter to ten!'

'Drink up, I said,' he hissed. In five minutes we were in another pub where Peel bought a double round of four pints. I then noticed he still had the ring. He smiled. 'Wanna buy one?' he inquired, as he produced half a dozen out of his top pocket. 'The only gold one is the one on my finger though the others have been dipped and stamped.' I was, to say the least, dumbstruck until I remembered his dubious friends in the 'Smoke'.

Finally the last week of our training arrived, after which we would all be posted to different regiments. The lads in the platoon decided we would have a really good night out on the Friday to celebrate. Then on the Thursday occurred one of the oddest incidents of my early time in the army. Old J. P., without a word of warning, or for that matter, goodbye, just disappeared from the face of the earth! I was never to see him again. During and after the war I made a few inquiries and tried to track him down but without any luck. The manageress of the pub where we had stayed was guarded when I contacted her, saying he had at least five names to her knowledge, one of which was John Peel. It appeared he would regularly join the services, mainly the army, to be, in her words, 'safe from society'. Still, whatever he had done and no doubt has done since, I never forgot him for being such a good mate to a naive youngster.

Despite Peel's disappearance, Friday night arrived and we all went down to a pub in Norwich where a good time was had by all. On the way back also came my opportunity to exact sweet revenge. As we staggered along in a large group, I noticed our room corporal straggling along in the rear rather the worst for ale. Alongside the road was a kind of man-made stream or gutter edged with low railings about eighteen inches high; the water was filthy. I had seen it every day when marching in and out of the barracks. Now it was absolutely pitch dark because of the blackout and I slowly let the rest of the lads overtake me as I sauntered drunkenly. I was soon in line with the corporal. Making sure he was looking the other way I gave him one almighty push and heard a splash, a curse and a shout. Quickly I caught up with the others and back at barracks, despite my glee, I never mentioned my 'achievement'. The next morning we were all out on parade waiting to hear about our postings. As I left the barrack room, I glanced at the corporal's uniform hanging by his locker. Sure enough, it was plastered in green moss and all kinds of flotsam. Oh, if only Peel had been there to see it!

5

Oh I do like to be beside the seaside

A S THINGS TURNED OUT, I was never posted away but stayed for a time at the Britannia Barracks with the Royal Norfolks. Most of the blokes were good sorts, mainly farmers' sons from Norfolk and Suffolk, and eventually we were joined by a few odd balls like me from Liverpool, Birmingham, Bristol and a couple of southern cities. Life seemed one long series of exercises, forced marches, weapon training, initiative and battle courses, all very easy but tiresome, Eventually one day we were all shown a film about the other activities we could elect to do, usually for extra pay. The latter triggered my imagination and so I chose the parachute training, hoping in the end to join a para brigade. I duly had to take a test and, once I passed, I was interviewed by a major. He seemed like my first real soldier: medal ribbons, leather-covered cane, the lot—relaxed yet obviously efficient. He had a slight Scottish accent and chain-smoked as he took down endless particulars about my past life, my father's occupation, his war service in the Great War, my mother and so on. I was becoming exasperated as he then asked about my grandparents. I replied I had only known one, my grandma or 'Ninny', who had lived with us until her death but, I added, to the best of my knowledge, all four were safely ensconced in Ford Cemetery and doubted they would be of any real use to the war effort unless the country ran short of fertiliser.

At this point he burst out laughing and drew the interview to a close, wishing me luck. I returned to my regiment and had all the particulars, especially that about the extra pay, entered on AB64 Part One. I was only back at barracks a month when the call came to go to Sherringham. It turned out to be a lovely little place on the east coast where the army

Training over, 'Posted to Royal Norfolk Regiment', Rookie Days.

had commandeered all of the main hotel. All kinds of characters from various ranks were breezing in and out. After reporting to the desk, I was shown to a small top-floor room which had two wooden beds; then the usual paraphernalia followed about collecting biscuits, pillow etc. By the time I got back to the room I found I was sharing with a full corporal, later nicknamed 'Two Stripes', who had already made up his bed; initially I just assumed he was on the staff until he said he had only arrived about an hour before. He was a Geordie and by then I had come to like them as warmhearted realists so we hit it off from the start. As we swapped stories about our training and backgrounds and when, if ever, we would get some grub, I noticed the door—'Heh mate, have you seen the door, no knob, no keyhole on this side.' We both had a go at opening it without success and things began to seem desperate when we both wanted the lavatory. We tried the window but it would not budge and there were thick bars on the outside.

Then the Geordie noticed the ceiling which had been recently plastered; all this was after three or four hours of shouting. 'Let's break the plaster,' he suggested, as we jumped on to the bunks and made a hole; lo and behold, there was a cockloft into which we climbed to find a trap door which led to the stairs outside the room. Geordie dropped down on to the landing first and within an instant we were joined by a lieutenant and a sergeant, both with broad smirks on their faces.

'Tea, gentlemen?' the lieutenant inquired, leading us into a cosy, carpeted lounge with a large settee, three enormous armchairs plus six dining tables all set for tea and covered, somewhat incongruously, with pink gingham tablecloths; a huge fireplace with logs set in a large polished wood surround dominated the room.

We were invited to sit at a table as the sergeant fetched a portfolio for the lieutenant. Two soldiers in white short coats and khaki uniforms pushed in a trolley heaving with meat sandwiches, shortbread and pots of tea. 'I'll be mother,' said the lieutenant, as we tucked into the veritable feast, 'you'll meet the rest of the crowd tomorrow. I've copies of your personal civvy and army histories in this file and want to interview you individually in due course. You will not be allowed out this evening but you can purchase drinks if you wish. I must insist that you never, ever, mention this room in any future conversations and if you do so, you will be RTU [Returned to unit]. Understood?' We nodded as it was obvious no explanation would be forthcoming.

We were then shown to our real sleeping quarters; they were pretty good by army standards, six single beds, the usual steel lockers and our very own washbasin. 'Here's a key each but we must insist that this room is never empty; one of you must stay here unless ordered otherwise.' 'More party games,' I thought, raising my eyebrows knowingly at Geordie.

'How about a pint?' he asked when we were alone.

'You go then, I'll stay. No doubt it's another "intelligence test".' Off he went. After ten minutes I was starting to doubt I would ever see anyone again when there was a knock.

'Who's there?'

In walked the sergeant.

'You can go and join the Geordie now in the bar if you like. You've passed your first test by staying put,' he announced with amusement. I was off like a shot, soon laughing with Geordie; kids' play and too many Hollywood films, we both agreed, though we made sure such comments were whispered. 'Watch out tomorrow, for God's sake, don't mention the lounge when we meet the others,' I hissed, 'one of them's bound to be a plant.'

'Shrewd, suspicious Scouser,' he chuckled.

'Better safe than sorry; when did you last get grub like today!?'

Breakfast, as we had been informed by a note left the previous evening, was at eight. The dining room, which of course we had to use our initiative to find, seated about fifty but I never saw it full. A brimming tea urn answered our immediate needs as did the mountains of bread and margarine. Meals later proved to have a good deal of variety and were a remarkable improvement on the barracks' rations. Breakfast over, there seemed to be no other choice but to return to our room where eventually the sergeant told us to fill in time sorting our kit until the afternoon. The party games continued.

'Under no circumstances must you leave the hotel, though you can have a look around the place,' he barked as we sighed. After he left and before Geordie could open his mouth I started, 'You go first and look around. I'm staying in the room like they said.' 'You're right, John, I'd already forgotten,' he mused. We took it in turns but there was not much to see; most of the doors were locked, even those purporting to lead to the games room and the garden. All the ground floor windows were fully sandbagged. I climbed up four flights of stairs, meeting five varieties of officer on the way. Bored with saluting, I returned to home base to find three other squaddies had arrived and sat in awkward silence with Geordie and the sergeant. There were no introductions. 'Lunch at 12.30 sharp,' he stated briskly as he rose to leave.

'I suppose the room's not to be left unoccupied?' I inquired. 'You suppose right,' he snapped back. 'You can talk about your past and present only in here, lads; casual gossip's the order of the day outside. We'll fill you in on the details later and though some of our rules might seem a bit soft, we don't want you to sit more than two to a table in the dining room. By the way, we're still waiting for one more bloke.'

Later, after lunch, and our final arrival, the lieutenant and the sergeant arrived. 'Sit on your beds and get comfy,' the sergeant announced as he sat at a small table which the room had mysteriously acquired during lunch. 'Right, we are a group of men who are going to be forged into one unit, but with all being able to operate independently of the rest when required. Let's get down to business. I want your AB64s, parts 1 and 2, plus your dog tags. Any questions?'

'What if we get picked up by MPs?' one guy asked as we all looked a bit suspicious about surrendering our ID cards and pay books plus our plastic discs. 'Why the hell should they? What are you thinking about getting up to?' the sergeant replied unsympathetically.

'Yeah, but what about if we had an accident?' another suggested more timidly.

'Don't worry. You'll only be alone when you visit the lav.'

'Do we get a receipt, you know, some proof?' I asked.

'They're all army property, not yours.' I wanted to debate this but thought better of it. 'You'll all have numbers depending on your order of arrival; I'm, number one, the lieutenant,

15 cwt truck, main transport for our group.

two, Geordie, Three and so on.' Thus I was four, a chap from
Woodbridge, Suffolk, five, another from Dundalk, six, a second
Geordie, seven, and a Londoner, eight. 'Each of your numbers
is to be followed by the letter 'D' and I'm going to give you
some nicknames; the lieutenant and I will just use our ranks,
Geordie and Scouser are self evident.' The guy from Suffolk
was to be Poacher, the Irishman predictably Paddy, the second
Geordie Gypsey, and the Londoner, Spud. Gypsey objected
vehemently but sat in thunderous silence when he was threatened with RTU. 'Right,' the sergeant moved on, 'you'll all
have to learn a lot, to drive, use maps and compasses effectively,
first and, above all, how to use a wireless.'

Thus we passed our time from October 1942 to August
1943. I really enjoyed it when we were all taken out in a 15 cwt
truck and dropped in the wilds of Norfolk or Suffolk, mainly
in the middle of the night. We were then given a time by
which to return to the hotel and an emergency phone number
if necessary. On four occasions we parachuted into Norfolk
on moonless nights and had to make it back to base as specified.

This was not only a stimulating challenge to lads of our age
but nearly always a good laugh as things never went smoothly
and we developed a ready line of patter for both the civilians
and the military police we met. We, in pre-SAS style, had to
live off the land, but it was amazing how many farmers and
others gave us drinks once they were reassured we were only
on exercises. We were never questioned about our ID while
everywhere posters warned about fifth columnists and careless
talk costing lives.

Overall physical training was given a very high priority;
running, climbing and unarmed combat took up a good deal
of time, the latter being a great safety valve for all of us to
let of steam as niggardly arguments did tend to surface given
our social confines.

Once trained to his satisfaction, the lieutenant then called
a meeting to explain our first task, a real job. 'We are to act
as a liaison team with our American allies,' he stated in his

BBC voice tinged with a little sarcasm. 'In the interests of entente cordial and an effective united war effort, we are to visit various camps and regiments, mainly Yank, to demonstrate our military hardware: some of our small arms, Sten gun, Bren and Piat etc. Then our allies will do us the courtesy of explaining some of theirs. Any questions?'

Silence. It all sounded a cushy number. So started a spate of nationwide tours of US bases and a good time was generally had by all, once, that is, we had got over our first encounter with our cousins from 'across the pond'.

One infamous trip was to a base in Sunningdale where with other ranks we were taken to a Nissen hut and treated with embarrassing, incomprehensible deference by several American lads, all with combat haircuts, real 'tough cookies'. It was

Fully trained soldier.

nearly lunchtime and the Yankee NCO explained his guys would be ready for the lecture at 2.30 p.m. if we would like to eat first. The dining hall was superb, a huge room seating at least four hundred, covered in quite proficient wall paintings of famous pin up girls. Above all, it was light and bright. Down one side were hundreds of hotplates where food was being served, canteen style, by black Americans. We noticed the indented trays at the end of the queue, put two and two together, and joined the line. (In our canteens, two separate plates was the norm for the two courses.) Already we were salivating; the food smelt and looked one hundred per cent better than anything we had had for weeks.

'You can have as much as you want, Limey,' one Yank shouted, 'no rationing here!'

'Fill it up, then,' said Joe our corporal cheerfully to a some-what wary black cook. So he did and so did the next guy; before he had time to blink, the second cook dumped rice and jam right on top of his roast dinner.

'What the fuckin' hell are you playing at?' Joe screamed, jumping on the hotplate and emptying the plate over the of-fending confused cook. Quickly an American NCO stepped in to cool things down and then our own lieutenant and sergeant plus an American colonel came over to explain if we wanted separate courses we should, as usual put plates on our trays as otherwise it all came en masse. It turned out that some poorer US recruits were quite happy with that arrangement.

After this, Joe went straight back to apologise and shake hands with the cook; in an instant I experienced the ugly stench of racial prejudice for the first time; all the white yanks started booing Joe loudly. With sophisticated disdain, we all ignored them.

After the meal, the yanks stated they wanted us to explain the Piat anti-tank gun first and here Joe, still a little raw from his lunchtime frolics, came into his own; although none of us were bullshitters he thought it would be a good idea if we acted like the stereotyped barrack room soldiers while the yanks began to amble and slouch on to the field. The lieutenant was all for a few minutes of amateur dramatics; Joe sprang into action, marching with expert briskness, stamping his feet as hard as he could and yelling, 'Company on parade!' The remaining six of us stomped out with weapons, lined up smartly as Joe brought us to attention, marched over to the lieutenant, saluted and yelled even more loudly, 'Company ready for your inspection, Sir!' The lieutenant reciprocated and came over for a textbook inspection; he took over, ordered a left turn as we went down the field like the 'Trooping of the Colour' and halted with immediacy that even impressed us. Our allies were gobsmacked, with a really embarrassed officer, but we could tell they thought we were zombies. We then went through our act with so much professionalism that, by the end, the air hung heavy with silent respect. All in all our stay went well and did much to build bridges; we enjoyed every minute, especially those spent in the canteen where the cuisine was superb.

Our next major assignment, shrouded in the accepted secrecy, took us to Tilbury Docks. We were herded into the usual 15 cwt truck, stopping at various army camps on the way for rations and refreshments; at one we handed in our .303 rifles which were replaced by the Sten guns we kept throughout our service. On arriving at

Training on the river Thames. I hated every minute.

Tilbury, we were met by an officer and an NCO who exchanged documents with our number one; we were then ushered along the dock to a shed which was to house us and our kit for the next six months. The 15 cwt truck was duly removed and we settled down into quite a routine; we took it in turns for two of us to guard our stuff in the shed while the rest went out on manoeuvres. These involved spending a good deal of the time on an old barge with a crusty Cockney 'captain', a nice old guy who was well trained in asking no questions and so used our accents to identify us. He was an incredible character with a perverse sense of humour. We would sail up and down the Thames nearly every day and on occasions even ventured out to sea. This was not my cup of tea at all; I felt permanently nauseous and was always glad to be back on terra firma. Every now and again our Cockney would drop an inflatable dinghy and give us instructions to board a selected ship and return with proof of our success. We did pretty well and viewed the whole operation as yet more army games. I did, however, make several unsuccessful trips into London in search of J. P.

Finally in February 1944 we were posted back to the 'real' British army in Colchester, delivered again by 15 cwt truck. Here some mail caught up with me, including a week-old letter from my Mam in Liverpool. Although she tried in her clumsy way to tone down her anxiety, it was obvious that my Dad was seriously ill and she herself was worried sick. Straightaway I went to our lieutenant. 'Look,' I said, upset yet surprisingly businesslike, 'I haven't ever asked any favours and I can't remember that much leave lately but I've got to go home. I think my ole fella's dying. I must get home.'

'I'll make enquiries and let you know,' he replied, with obvious reservations about my chances of success. Two days later, a Thursday I recall, he sent for me. 'No can do,' he said, 'too much's building up and all routine leave has been cancelled.'

'Look, I've just got to get home and I don't care how. Is there any senior officer who could use his bloody discretion or something?'

'Seriously no; I'd like to help. If you're determined to do something stupid, I don't know if I'll be able to bail you out but here's a phone number to contact me or leave me a message in an emergency. We'll be here for at least another week,' he replied, passing me a small piece of card.

I later jumped camp, bought a platform ticket and freeloaded a ride to London where it would simply be a matter of changing trains. I made my way to Euston and boarded a Liverpool train, praying I would escape the examiners or wartime ticket inspectors who were usually kept busy on crowded long-distance trains. I passed through Rugby with safety but by the time we had left Crewe, the word went round that the examiners were on board and heading my way. I sauntered along to the toilets with several other squaddies. The idea was to cram as many soldiers into a cubicle as possible so that when the examiner knocked, one ticket only would be shoved under the door. Obviously this worked well if you were with a group of pals and had clubbed together for one ticket but sometimes comrades would squeeze one more in. I knocked on two without luck and then to my horror, I saw the examiner coming my way. I made one last effort at a toilet with no success and then lost my cool, 'Examiner!' I shouted. 'Pass your ticket under the door!' I was duly obeyed and picked up my prize. I walked towards the inspector, showed him the ticket and when he did not even bother to punch it I tried to get back to the loo but he beat me to it. I moved off quickly though the incident has been on my conscience ever since.

We were now approaching Edge Hill and here the train routinely slowed down in its approach to Liverpool Lime Street. A good many ticketless soldiers jumped off here and I decided to do the same as I had no leave warrant and Lime Street permanently crawled with police and 'red caps'. I dashed home and was surprised to hear my father was at work. 'He's weak, John, but he says he's feeling better and as he's on shifts now, he should be home after 10 o'clock,' my mother explained, worry etched deep into her face.

'I'm going down straight away; they're probably be okay about me seeing him if I explain about my leave.' I got down to the factory, the Liverpool Scotch Feather company in Blackstock Street about 9.30 p.m. I explained I was on short leave and could someone tell my Dad I'd be waiting for him outside. 'Go on in now, lad,' said the guy on the door, 'he's down the stairs in the boiler room in the yard.'

I had no trouble finding it but the factory had not moved on since the nineteenth century. The air was thick with feathers and tiny white particles of moist dust as I choked and spluttered my way to the staircase. To be fair, Dad's boiler room seemed to be healthiest spot in the whole set up. Dad's face lit up as I entered the room but I struggled not to show the shock I felt at the change in him. He looked drained, grey and worn. There was another bloke with him who turned out to be his relief; after the usual introductions he volunteered to take over early. 'No point hangin' around, fellas, you've got a lot of catching up to do. You'll just be in time to have a pint.' We walked as quickly as Dad could to the pub at the corner of Blackstock Street and Vauxhall Road where we knew the manager, Bill Moore, an ex-copper. Both Dad and I seemed pleased with ourselves; he was made up to see me and I was proudly aware that this was the first time I had been out drinking with him.

'Your lad seems a bit young for the army,' Moore commented. 'Bloody fool signed up early and lied about his age; gets it from his mother's side,' Dad retorted. We caught up on general news and swapped stories about events since we had last met but I could not help thinking about how ill he looked; a grey pallor seemed ingrained on a face now tired and worn. I felt a sense of something ebbing away, beyond my control as I slowly walked back along Vauxhall Road with him. As I feared, it turned out to be the only drink I ever had with him; he died shortly after, the first death to really get to me, as it still does, despite the later loss of friends and family.

The next day I rang the lieutenant at Colchester barracks and was lucky to be put through to him. 'I'm in Liverpool and me dad's really bad but I'll be back tonight or at the latest some time on Monday morning sir,' I explained hastily.

'How much was the fare or did you use your initiative?' he replied quite warmly.

'My initiative, sir.'

'Well, let's hope you get back without incident.' He was, as we all thought, a good bloke and tried twice on later occasions to get me leave without success.

6

La Belle France

SOON after a rather uneventful return journey to Colchester, our band of merry men was moved to Bognor Regis. By now it was early in the March of 1944 and I still have fond memories of the birthday I spent there. The army had, as might be expected, commandeered most of the hotels and boarding houses along the front. Ignoring a beach packed with scaffolding, barbed wire and various anti-Gerry devices (even mines were rumoured), the town seemed a most pretty place; even the buildings' faded paintwork added a touch of elegant dignity in the spring sunshine. The few locals we met were genuinely friendly and helpful; the air was thick with speculation about the invasion and this dominated conversations with the town's inhabitants. We were as much in the dark as anyone and joked each time we were asked about seeing Churchill that evening at dinner. The town did seem a hive of military activity, however low key they tried to keep it. Lorries, tanks and streams of troops and equipment seemed to be permanently in transit. We carried on with what seemed by then to be routine training but our moods varied between dejected boredom and irritable expectation.

Then, all of a sudden on 1 June, we were told to get ready to leave. All our equipment was loaded on to the statutory 15 cwt truck and then we appeared to travel about six or seven miles to an army camp-come-RAF camp. We were shown to the usual home from home, a nissen hut set up for thirty men. In the end two other groups of ten arrived in addition to our team of eight. We were ordered briskly to march to the dining room and told to stay at our tables, one for each team, unless we wanted to go to the lavatory. We were given fifteen minutes to settle down, after which all the tables were cleared and on ominous looking envelope was placed on each. Silence followed but yet another ten minutes seemed to elapse during which the tension steadily mounted. Faces showed the strain of apprehension. Our lieutenant tried to break the ice.

'Any guesses where we are?' he asked with a smile. Before anyone could reply, we were all summoned somewhat dramatically to attention; instant pandemonium was stillborn as tables and chairs thundered for a split second. The door opened and in walked four officers, three captains and a lieutenant colonel.

'Right men, sit down and get comfortable. This could take some time so smoke if you wish,' said the commanding officer. The lights were turned on and the windows shuttered from the inside. We heard someone barking orders outside and found out later that an armed security guard had surrounded the building. A huge map was placed on one wall showing a section of the French coast; the main towns were clearly marked, Lion-sur-Mer, Ouistreham, Hermanville and Benonville as were various crossroads and observation points, gun emplacements and distinguishing features of the local countryside. A lecture was then given by the lieutenant colonel, who stressed how lucky we were to be picked for this operation; the captains then explained in laborious detail all the map's important features, emphasising how important it would be to capture and/or destroy all the salient spots so that future operations could benefit from our knowledge and experience. After what seemed like near on three hours, there was the usual 'any questions' session in which, in true army style, most answers were negative or the phrase about 'further details to be issued later' was ambiguously mentioned. We were finally informed that we were confined to barracks for the rest of our stay, to get as much sleep and rest as possible and that local group commanders would be able to open envelopes once we returned to our quarters.

On dismissal, we rushed back to our bunks eager to know our fate. The lieutenant produced our targets, Lion-sur-Mer and Hermanville, including all relevant crossroads, observation posts and anything on the beach of use to Gerry.

Instructions re various map references and dropping zones were issued as was the order to create as much havoc as possible once we had completed these motifs. We all carefully examined and discussed the prospect before us; by now we were almost automatically thinking as one being with a multiple personality. We heard planes rumbling overhead, US Dakotas and later were introduced to our Yankee crew who were to drop us in France. They were then taken to their sleeping quarters.

We spent the next two days testing our weapons and equip ment with a new earnestness; despite the regular flow of witticisms, our collective mood oscillated between nervous excitement, brooding boredom and moments of cold fear. The lieutenant told us exactly what to pack, the rest of our stuff was to be placed in army stores. We were allowed to write one letter home with no mention of our position or movements. All such correspondence was naturally left opened for the censor. Again, somewhat ominously church services were announced, the eleven Roman Catholics in the groups were to hear Mass at the end of the nissen hut. All of them except me received Holy Communion as I had a mental block to the idea that such a gesture by a baptised heathen would do any good. Needless to day, the priest, nice guy though he was, collared me about it at the end. I said some day I might see the light on the road to Damascus and he laughed, shook hands and blessed me.

When we all got back together, about four in the afternoon, we agreed the whole show had to be starting pretty soon; we were informed that tea would be late that day but to get some sleep. In the end tea turned into a splendid roast lamb dinner at 7.30 p.m. while no one had slept a wink all day. A rumour flew round the canteen that we were all to be shipped off to another camp.

'I wish they'd make up their bloody minds!' stammered Paddy in genuine frustration. We were all ushered back to our sleeping quarters by 9.30 p.m., thoroughly fed up. We went through the motions of getting ready to settle down for the night when about 10.15 p.m. the lieutenant colonel entered the room with a major and a regimental sergeant major. The latter told us to stay as we were and listen to the senior officer, who came straight to the point.

'Right, within three hours you will all be dropped in France. You have had plenty of time to study your maps and targets. I want you now to start preparing yourselves for the drop. Do not forget to have a wash and shave before you get 'corked up'. I wish you the best of luck, gentlemen.'

As he left the major gave the three unit commanders another envelope each, to be opened on the plane. Trucks arrived for all twenty-eight of us at 11.45 to take us to our aircraft. Our group was to be the first to drop. It was only then the sheer amount of stuff we were taking struck me as we packed into the Dakota. We all shuffled nervously as the engines revved up and off we took. It seemed funny now but during training I had always imagined catching my first glimpse of the Channel but I could not see anything; that would have to wait for future holidays abroad! We generally got the impression we were over the coast once the flak from the German anti-aircraft batteries started. Our group was told to get ready as the door and our mouths opened, stomachs sank and we were all 'hooked up' waiting for an almost unreal green light. Away we went; the whole experience was so overwhelming it was difficult to later recall any particular emotion. The sky was incredible, full of the swaying red lights of tracer bullets. All too soon I hit the ground. God, in retrospect, was I lucky! I landed in a field near a stone wall. I quickly took off my surplus equipment, burying some under the earth; I examined my map and reference bearing and took compass readings. It appeared I was not too far from our rendezvous point. In celebration I had a drink of water from my water bottle, my mouth dry with tension. I felt very alone for the first time in months. I thought of the others and the chats we had had as we had learned to live in each other's pockets. Gypsey kept coming into my mind's eye; it had become apparent that five out of the six of us squaddies had shared common lifestyles in back-to-back inner-city poverty, Gypsey being the exception. Naturally reticent, he was a stonewall for many months on this subject until he finally described his life as a traveller and once in a bout of homesickness even drew a superb picture of his family's colourful horse-drawn caravan. To him, the term 'gypsy' was anathema, tantamount to a racist label; in his own way he was the opposite of the bigoted stereotype of travellers, being fearlessly honest in all matters.

With such thoughts I carefully attempted to find my rendezvous point at the crossroads near Hermanville's left junction towards the coast. I had a mile to cover according to my information. The night was dark with the occasional burst of moonlight. I moved on with little real trouble as our planes provided a major distraction for the German anti-aircraft gunners who had started to sound trigger happy by this point in the night. Slowly I passed a couple of houses and crossroads. Although risky, I was glad to be out of the ankle deep mud that had accompanied most of my walk thus far. I crossed the road with precautionary haste to the rubble of several demolished buildings. Once clear of the debris I decided to take a chance and call out our code. To make matters more hairy, this had to be repeated three times before anyone would reply. What a feeling when Poacher gave out the agreed response. It turned out he had been watching me for a while and soon Gypsey, Paddy and Geordie emerged from some nearby bushes. An hour later Spud finally arrived but the sergeant and the lieutenant never turned up. We were never to discover their fate but that night we hoped for the best for them. We had been trained to act as a team, to make collective decisions without the necessity of higher ranks so we decided, as day was breaking, to make our position more secure, to spread out but keep each other in view; we then would try to survey any possible targets but remain relatively inactive during daylight. Now all we needed was our wireless call giving us the go ahead. We had been warned that if no message came within forty-eight hours to make our own way back to allied territory but not to stay in France. Would you believe it! Reminiscent of later war films, we had lost the damned wireless but we knew that eventuality had been covered. We were to wait for coloured flares dropped by passing aircraft. We spent a very boring, nervous 5 June waiting but picking up useful information about the movement and routine of the locals and the Gerries.

As darkness fell, we regrouped, pooled our knowledge and decided that the set targets would take between two and three hours to hit. Apart from the usual communications, gun batteries, railway lines and signals, our main hit was to be the German observation post overlooking Lion-sur-Mer. We reckoned there were about forty Germans involved and we felt our prayers were answered when we saw most of them retiring to a bunker as night fell, leaving only three guarding the post. We slowly moved closer during the night but disaster nearly struck when a local dog barked and attacked Gypsey, delivering several vicious bites before it met its end. A German soldier was roused to open the post's door and shout at the dog but then went back inside unconcerned.

Daylight again broke amidst a backdrop of a never-ending air raid. Tiredness was now noticeably taking its toll but we got our second wind once we saw the coloured flares. Three of us went straight to the post to find two Germans fast asleep while the duty officer dozed. Needs must as the devil drives and we quickly disposed of them. We destroyed all the relevant equipment; we felt jubilant at the speed, the lack of noise and the fact that we had not fired a shot. We were about to make for the bunker when we spotted a German officer and squaddie

making straight for the post. Quickly we shut the door and
again silently they met their end as they entered. Using a
telescope and binoculars we looked towards Lion-sur-Mer and
the mist which shrouded the Channel. Our three mates had
already 'bottled up' the bunker by simply clamping down the
outside handles. It would be some time before the crowd inside
were rescued, if ever. Thus we made our way to Lion-sur-Mer
but were under orders not to enter the town itself. We picked
off a few targets en route, including a succession of military
vehicles, petrol and communication dumps. Then, to use a
hack phrase, 'the balloon went up' with coastal bombardment
on a scale that could not fail to impress. We used our binoculars
to be awed by the sheer number of ships. Impressive though
it was, this was no time to hang about as we were being shelled
as much as the Gerries. We edged towards Hermanville where,
at the crossroads we spotted our first impromptu sitting duck,
a convoy of three lorries and a staff car, too good to be missed.
We rapidly took up our positions either side of the road and
gave some of them the last shock of their lives; two lorries
were 'taken out' while the others did a quick turn round back
to the town. Here, too, we suffered our first loss; Geordie was
hit and there was little we could do apart from cover his body.
In the heat of the moment were were jolted by the shock but
grief would come later. By this point I spotted Gypsey limping
badly; he said the dog had done its damage. 'Let's have a
look,' I offered.

'Fuck off! There'll be time for that at Hermanville,' he
snapped. Then all hell broke out as we came under fire from
some Germans with a spandau machine gun. Gypsey and
Poacher indicated they would work around to the left and take
them from behind while we gave them covering fire. Poacher
with surprising speed signalled their success and we rushed
to meet them only to find Gypsey dead, dead! Coming so soon
after Geordie, I could not handle it. It was about 5.30; we had
been going for a nerve-racking twenty-four hours. We took
time out to bury him, safer than we had been with poor old

Geordie. We marked the spot; the idea of a later, decent burial seemed to consume us.

Once calm after a fashion we spotted what seemed like a German retreat from Hermanville as fighter planes, mainly Yank, buzzed overhead. We stopped in a copse, collected our thoughts and kept still, seeing the crossroads, our supposed destination some three hundred yards away. The Gerries seemed to be panicking and in cold anger we decided to help them along. Taking up sniper positions, we started picking them off with considerable success. They just did not seem to want to fight back; retreat was their highest priority. We decided to improve our chances by moving to higher ground;

These planes were not shot down, but shot up on the ground.

it seemed a good time as dusk descended. Of course, it was our fatal mistake induced by cocksure complacency. We literally walked into a bunch of Germans with the statutory spandau. There was no choice, we just had to go towards the fire. Spud and Poacher went down quickly, best mates as nine pins, by the time we got the gun, one Gerry lay dying; it is hard to come to terms with the human damage you inflict. He tried to speak a little in English as he passed away. All I could get, I think, was that he was not German but Polish. Paddy and I jumped into the trench for cover, pulling Spud and Poacher with us. By now it was dark and in our state it seemed wise to wait and rest in silence until daybreak. Lying there during those sleepless hours I thought I would crack. I decided I had lost all sanity when I heard a Scouse accent. It was about four or five in the morning on 7 June. I lightly tapped Paddy who claimed he was snoozing but seemed to be in a similar mindless trance. 'I'm listening!' he whispered sharply. 'I hear a Scouse,' I offered.

'I think you're right; we'll wait till daylight to be sure.'

At sunrise, again the binoculars came out. Amid continued sporadic firing there were without   ubt, some British troops, a mere fifty yards away, but it was impossible for them to see us.

'What about a white flag? Or should I just take a chance and shout?'

'Listen, this is probably the only time in your life that your bloody accent is going to come in handy. Shout, they're bound to recognise your twang,' he whispered back, evidently in better humour. Thus I shouted though I cannot remember the exact words.

'Where are you from?' Came the reply.

'Liverpool.' I yelled.

'Oh yer, whereabout?' Jesus, I thought, what do they want, a lesson in urban geography!

'Scottie Road.'

'Come on down, no weapons.'

'All right, there's two of us, coming down now.'

'No, just you.'

I stood up with some trepidation, hands in the air and walked to meet them. What a reception! It was like coming home. Paddy never waited for his invite but just came running with excitement. The guys were from the South Lancs Regiment and nearly all were Scousers. After a couple of minutes of euphoria, we mentioned Poacher and Spud; without any fuss some came with us and we buried two more good mates. We were then interviewed by their captain and moved up the line with surprising speed to their HQ. Here the welcome was overwhelming as we emerged probably from a state of shock. We washed and shaved. Then, at last, were given spam, biscuits and a big mug of tea. Thank God! Sadly we were both given a packet of cigarettes; without thinking I took one out, lit up and promptly coughed my head off. 'You don't smoke!' Paddy stared in disbelief.

'Looks like I do now,' I replied with wry humour. It has proven to be a lifelong problem ever since. At this point Paddy mentioned his leg to the major who was interviewing us. I had a few cuts but was shocked to watch him show a very deep four-inch gash just above his knee, dressed sloppily in a dirty field dressing. With yet more impressive speed we were moved along with some other wounded chaps towards the beach and transport home.

It was with mixed emotions that we watched the French coastline disappear and with it six of the best pals we would ever have. Despite repeated inquiries both then and in the years afterwards, I never found out the fate of the lieutenant and the sergeant. Gypsey, Geordie, Poacher and Spud were finally interred with some dignity in a proper war cemetery in France. Even now the memories cause pain; readers might well criticise me for not having described them more fully, more individually in an earlier chapter, but it is difficult to write about their humour, their kindness and then their sudden deaths. D-Day taught me to understand what a truly

professional soldier means when he emphasises his dislike of
war, of clearing up, perhaps with his life, a mess created by
years of political one-upmanship and complex, often hypo-
critical, diplomacy. I never understood why men had to die
in the First War. Intellectually, in my mind, I can rationalise
why the evils of fascism had to be stopped in the Second, but,
then, in my heart, I remember the six of them and bite my
lip in silent grief.

7

Blighty and more holidays abroad!

WE DISEMBARKED at Folkstone and were sent to a makeshift hospital where we got five-star treatment, warm baths, a comfy ward, a hearty meal and lots of tea. I kept protesting I only had a couple of scratches but no one seemed interested. Paddy and I had not spoken for hours; the air hung heavy with guilt.

Slowly, hesitatingly, we stumbled across our feelings; why us, not them, luck of the draw, fortunes of war, it should have been us—the same points, the same pain, then sleep. The next day we initially could not recall our conversation. I think we had been heavily sedated because we had slept like lambs for well over ten hours. The medical staff, as ever, continued to be marvellous but by the afternoon the treat was over. New uniforms were provided and we were told we would be moving on. We were collected by a captain in a chauffeur-driven small canvas-topped van, known as a P.U. and taken to a rather grand old house outside Deal. Here three officers interviewed us intensively, one by persistently referring to the map of our activities. We started to get as upset as was permissible for ordinary squaddies. We kept saying we had told them all we could remember, that it had not been a happy time. One officer was kind and considerate but kept repeating, 'Come on lads, just one more time, war is war.' By the end we felt like rung-out rags.

'Look,' I said, 'Any chance of a night out and a few bob.
Christ, I think we deserve it.'

'All's being arranged,' came the warm reply.

Paddy and I were then handed two temporary pay books
plus a fiver each. We were driven to Deal, the driver choosing
the pub, and given a number to phone when we wanted collecting. As we got inside, Paddy was insistent we went to the
gents. He hissed almost hysterically, 'I'm fed up being ordered
here, ordered there, watched and told what to do all the bloody
time. We'll check to see the driver's gone and then make a
quick exit for a pub of our choice!'

'Okay, okay.' I thought it was a good idea but was a bit
concerned about his mood.

Fairly sharpish, we slipped out of a side door, down a couple
of back streets and into a cosy little hostelry packed, as ever,
with service personnel. With five quid each, we indulged in
some heavy drinking and Paddy's mood mellowed rather than
lightened. 'I'm going to ask for leave when we get back!' he
announced, his tone implying 'ask' meant 'demand'. I agreed
to keep him happy and because it seemed only fair. What
happened after that is a bit of a blur; to say we got drunk is
the understatement of Operation Overlord. We were a bit
vague about events after that. It seems we staggered into the
local police station at midnight and asked them to ring our
collection number. Presumably somebody must have picked
us up. We woke up back in the big house, washed and break-
fasted and then enjoyed the luxuries of the British press. The
news seemed good. At last the war seemed to be going our
way. Two officers paid us a visit and straightaway Paddy
carried out his threat. 'How about some leave, Sir?' He asked
one of them.

'Not yet, I'm afraid, perhaps in a few weeks when things
settle down in France. We need experienced chaps like your
good selves; we had rather more casualties than anticipated,'
came the reply. We thought about our casualties. We were
both angry but Paddy showed it.

'Well, what if we'd not come back? You wouldn't have missed us!' He blurted.

'But you did! I can't over-emphasise the importance of your experience. Surely you want revenge for your comrades?'

'Men with revenge in their hearts make dodgy fighters,' I interrupted, remembering, ironically, one of our lieutenant's training courses.

'Look, we need "volunteers" but you know we can still order you if we like. Play it our way and we'll get you leave as soon as we can.'

We accepted the offer, we knew we had very little choice. We spent several seemingly endless weeks in Deal till late

Relaxing. (Lemonade only.) Awaiting return to France.

August reassembling our kit and replacing that lost in France.
We were, as ever, just settling down into a routine when we
were moved on, this time to Dover, yet another house on
another seaside front with enough service personnel to give
the local pubs a roaring trade. Paddy was getting increasingly
restless, repeating how we could have had leave after all instead
of messing around in Dover. Finally, on 10th September, an
officer and sergeant disturbed our monotony and told us to
be ready to move at 1800 hours. We put all our kit into a
three-ton lorry with about twenty other squaddies and we were
chauffeured to Newhaven. Here we were issued with haversack
rations and within an hour we boarded a landing craft packed
with reinforcements for Europe. On board a major explained
that we would be joining another group to carry out the type
of 'disruptive' duties in which we had indulged in June.

We disembarked at Ouistreham, which brought memories
flooding back. Paddy and I were amazed at all the devastation.
It made it easier to understand why some of the French had
openly stated that they preferred the Gerries to us. Once
loaded, our convoy of lorries were driven through scenes of
scarred shambles as we proceeded through France, Belgium
and Holland, stopping only twice for rations. The convoy was
in a state of permanent shrinkage as lorries were periodically
redirected to various regiments. Paddy and I were dropped at
a place called Herentals where we met up with a couple of
other chaps and an officer who showed us to our 'quarters',
a cellar in a bombed out building. It had been made surprisingly
cosy and there we were to stay a couple of days awaiting
further orders. The others left first and then Paddy and I were
told we too would be moving behind German lines with some
armoured corps who were, to all intentional purposes, resting
overnight.

Thus, as it grew dark, we were placed with a tank regiment.
We had not a clue where we were. Paddy asked a sergeant
and a lieutenant, only to be told quite firmly that all would
be revealed the next day. Some chaps had erected a makeshift

tarpaulin 'tent' hanging from the side of their tank and they sportingly asked us to join them for a brew. We were then told to make ourselves comfortable and to get 'dug in' for the night; luckily there were plenty of empty slit trenches.

The next morning we were informed by an officer fluent in Dutch that we were going to Eindhoven, still in enemy hands. The big shock was that it was only to be Paddy and myself. The officer, seeing our surprise, hastily added, 'Plus, of course, the South African.'

The South African? This mystery man was eventually introduced to us. (He was already known to me, but that is another story). He knew Eindhoven well, having spent some of his childhood there before his parents emigrated to South Africa. He had even been back a couple of times on pre-war holidays. His greatest talent was that he could speak fluent German.

Our orders were to follow the railway lines into Eindhoven and wait for a contact alongside the nearby Phillips factory. We were a bag of nerves throughout the journey, which was surprisingly uneventful, apart from the usual backdrop of bombing. The South African soon earned Paddy's respect, excelling in all his tasks and showing no apparent fear. It was his job to introduce us to our first friends in the Dutch resistance. The first two took us to the Phillips factory where we met a third who smuggled us into the building itself. We all shook hands and went down to a kind of basement workshop where, in an adjoining room, another two guys were brewing coffee and encouraged us to have what we thought was battered fried fish; it turned to be some kind of fried bread filled with jam, all deliciously welcome with the hot drink. In the end there were seven of us. The South African was in charge and explained our duties and routines. The Dutch could speak fairly good English and had a wireless, which seemed appropriate in a Phillips factory—no problem with spare parts and little chance of Gerry detecting it! We were given a stern warning never to leave the room on our own; there were people working in the place day and night and the Germans kept a garrison of twenty to thirty men on the premises at all times. Two of the Dutch guys said they would provide all the rations. It was our job when ordered to stop the Gerries blowing up the research department before they retreated. Here it was suspected that advanced technical research was being under-taken on precision instruments for aircraft. We were then instructed in the plans and layout of the building, discussing the best positions to take up when the need arose. The bombing and shelling meanwhile seemed a permanent fact for life.

We spent a good few hours killing time by monitoring German movements until 15th September when the bombing seemed to step up a pace or two. Stuck down in the basement, we were told that fighter planes were also buzzing around. This was a good sign of an imminent land attack. Sure enough, the South African instructed us to take up our positions that night. The Gerries appeared in a state of hyperactive panic, barking orders and running round like headless chickens; it looked as though they were looting as much as they could before the retreat. In the end it was all a bit of a non-event as they never bothered us. We stayed in position throughout the 16th and on the 17th Gerry appeared to have gone. Feeling somewhat surplus to requirements, we made our way back to the basement. Here the Dutch guys were really jubilant and amazed me by saying that because it was Sunday they would go to Mass. I always thought they would all be Protestants given my limited historical knowledge of William of Orange *et al.* 'Are you Catholic?' I asked.

'Yes, sure and them too,' one replied gesticulating towards his mates. Paddy was 'made up'. Mass. Old habits die hard with the Irish.

'Let's all go,' he offered enthusiastically.

'Look, let's not get carried away!' I hastily jumped in, 'It's still a bit risky. We'll wait till we get the all clear that Gerry's gone.'

Everyone soberly agreed and on the 18th British tanks rolled into Eindhoven. What a day! Happiness all round, beer swilling factory workers dancing round the building typified the scene. Even I was now in the mood for thanksgiving. The South African came too and afterwards outside the church thanked us. 'Although I am not of your religion I did enjoy the service.'

Then back to basics as we reported with the Dutch to a celebrating lieutenant. We were told we would be splitting into two groups and so Paddy and I said a rushed farewell to our mates in the resistance and the South African. As they were given a hurried tea we were told that there was a big battle going on along the lines and a lieutenant colonel said we were to make for Veghel and then Uden. Here we stayed and enjoyed our first relaxed meal in days. The next morning, the 20th, yet another officer informed us things were not going too well at Arnhem and that we would soon be on the move to Nijmegen. On reaching the outskirts of Grave we were told to await further orders. None came and we stared for hours at roads packed with tanks that scarcely moved. Many of the troops we were with, especially the American Airborne, became increasingly frustrated thinking of the time the British Airborne were having with the Gerries at Arnhem. More than enough has been said about this particular battle, but no one could put any blame for the disaster on either the ground forces or the airborne. They all did their duty. The odds were too great, the strategy misconceived.

After the evacuation of Arnhem, Paddy and I returned, yet again, to Eindhoven. Paddy and I were interviewed first and told we were getting some leave: Blighty beckoned! Paddy was even considering nipping over to Ireland. What a shock we got when we were informed it was to be Brussels. We placed most of our kit and weapons in store and were issued with some pay books and B.A.F.O. money in guilders. Off we went to Brussels in a T.C.V., picking up various squaddies on the way.

Brussels proved to be an eye opener, full of lovely buildings
in stark contrast to the devastation we now regarded as the
norm. The streets were buzzing with ordinary people going
about their business, doing amazingly normal things like shop-
ping. It could have been peace time. We were unloaded into
a large car park where we collected the addresses of our new
billets and luncheon vouchers for a restaurant for British
troops. Above it was the useful army field cashier's where we
could change our guilders for francs. Duly kitted with money,
we reported back to the car park for transport to our temporary
homes.

Paddy and I were luckily stationed in the same road, Defre
Avenue, Bruges, without doubt a residential area of some class.
With some trepidation I knocked on the door of a huge detached house and was welcomed by a maid who fleetingly
checked my papers. As I entered I felt like an intruder, my
heavy army boots thundering across a highly polished tiled
floor. She gestured for me to come upstairs to see my room
and I tried to say I should take off my boots. She laughed
good-naturedly and showed me to the bedroom door. I turned
the key, what a sight! It was the height of opulence by any
standards, let alone those of a kid from Scottie Road. The
carpets and furnishings were little short of beautiful; there
were two huge fitted white wardrobes with ornate mirrors, a
table and two chairs and a draped window overlooking a very
pretty garden, but there in pride of place stood my first four
poster bed complete with lace curtains and covered with em-
broidered scatter cushions. There was even an adjoining bathroom, again spotless. Oh, what luxury! I quickly organised a
bath and a change of underwear and got tarted up ready for
my first day out in Brussels. A sobering notice in English
pinned to the door curbed some of my excitement. It warned
British personnel to be on their best behaviour in these billets,
always to inform the owner when you were going out and, if
possible, when you would be returning, midnight being the
deadline for all British Cinderellas.

I went downstairs, gingerly looking for the maid, when I met a distinguished looking gentleman of about seventy-five, with grey hair and a waxed moustache. He walked very slowly with the aid of a stick. I tried to assist him, passing the time of day and asking if he could tell the maid I was going out and would be back between eleven and twelve that night. In broken English he replied warmly, 'Maid? I have no maid. Only I and my daughter live here but a lady comes in to help with cleaning and gardening in the mornings.'

I blushed as his daughter approached and he explained my error. We all laughed and I was relieved I had not caused offence. I apologised but she assured me none was necessary. Paddy was in the avenue waiting for me and we hitched a lift on one of the innumerable army trucks to downtown Brussels. Again we stared in disbelief at the unscathed buildings and statues and the big, modern 'Bon Marché' which appeared to be doing a roaring trade with service personnel. Again it struck me as somewhat incongruous that less than fifty miles away was the carnage of war. We went to the restaurant for lunch only to be pestered incessantly by girls and children asking for cigarettes and/or chocolate, even though everything seemed plentiful. We later discovered that there were shortages of soap, coffee, and general 'eatables' and that one could sell B.A.F.O. money for three to four times the amount it was worth in Belgian francs. The main unofficial currency seemed to be, as all over Europe, cigarettes. Paddy and I were even crazy enough to sit outside a café enjoying too many cognacs, only to flee inside after half an hour exhausted by the begging. There seemed to be plenty of servicemen trading but it was all new to novices like us, fresh from the lines.

Paddy's billet with a retired couple appeared to be as plush as mine and we regretted we only had five days to sight see and pub crawl Brussels. We decided on the last two days to spend a few hours with our hosts by way of thanks. After three days of unadulterated fun, we had the black market tagged with the sole intention of thanking those who had made

us so welcome. Paddy asked his couple if he could bring around
a friend for a farewell chat and I made similar arrangements.
In the meantime we had amassed soap, cigarettes, chocolate,
corned beef and, above all, coffee. We neatly made up two
parcels. The drink was even easier to obtain. On the fourth
night we arrived as arranged at Paddy's at 6.00 p.m. The old
couple welcomed us into their lounge and had even laid on
some of their own wine. We produced our parcel and as they
opened it, they quietly cried. It was very embarrassing and
touching. They repeatedly asked if we would get into trouble
and it took most of the evening to reassure them that we would
not. Then we attempted to chat as best we could but Paddy's
accent and mine proved comic to those who barely grasped
the King's English. Eventually I staggered home at 9.30 p.m.,
glad it was a short walk and then straight to bed as I was
'relaxed' to say the least.

The next evening it was my turn; it was almost like an exact
re-run of the previous night except this time we were in a
beautifully furnished basement. In an alcove there was a bed
concealed by some curtains. The daughter mentioned their
fear of air raids and this triggered off a general conversation
about our respective families and the war. The old chap began
to describe his experience of the Great War when, somewhat
suddenly, the daughter went upstairs. He apologised in broken
English that she had to have a cry as her husband had been
arrested by the Germans and placed in a labour camp.

At this point we agreed to drop the subject although the
old guy quickly explained that Brussels surrendered to the
enemy in what many agreed was a damage limitation exercise.
In response the Germans had left the city pretty much as they
had found it. The daughter reappeared, apologised for her
'silliness' and the party broke up about 10.30 p.m. Paddy had
overindulged and I had to help him back to his digs and deposit
him in his room. I even pinned a note on him reminding him
to be in the car park at 9.00 a.m. for our return journey to
Eindhoven.

Back at base, we were informed that we were to be returned to our original regiments which seemed a lifetime ago after our months of absence. We collected our kit, Paddy was going back to the R.E.M.E. and I was to rejoin the Royal Norfolks. We swore to keep in touch and swapped home addresses. It was a farewell drink though I think the powers that be planned it thus. Needless to say, like so many army friends, Paddy and I never met again. My last memory is of him waving as I jumped into a lorry with a bunch of other squaddies. 'Where are we off?' I shouted to the driver.

'Maastricht,' came the reply as my one remaining pal faded in the distance.

8

The Darkest Hour

A T Maastricht I was met by a corporal. 'Come on lad, we've got about a mile to go before home!' he shouted cheerfully. 'Where's 'home'? I asked.

'Ah, you're lucky there; we've just been relieved and are having a well-earned rest in a local mental asylum.'

'Sounds about right,' I muttered as he grinned good-naturedly.

Soon enough we arrived at a hugh wooden gate where he pulled a chain to ring a bell inside. Then the insert door briskly opened and in we went. It seemed uncharacteristically dark as I squinted to make out some buildings, a good many trees and a large wall along which we walked till we reached an impressive iron gate. This was swiftly opened and closed by the chap on guard. We then entered one of the main buildings used by the squaddies. There were no beds but palliasse along the floor in four neat rows of fourteen. This, it turned out, was for 'A' Company of the Royal Norfolks. I did not know a soul but everyone was very friendly. They had all been there for three days and after some grub and a chat I was glad to get my head down after the night before.

The next day I was up and shaved, ready for breakfast and feeling a new man. Mess tins were the order of the day as we lined up outside, collected our tea in one tin and bread and bacon in the other, then back inside for fairly rapid consumption. My brief time in the queue allowed me a chance to get my bearings in the morning light. I saw the iron gate, about twelve foot high adjoining a wall about fifty yards long which separated our buildings from the main asylum. Ours was obviously what had been the administrative block while further on down you could see the asylum proper, built to hold several hundred inmates. On their side there was a kind of tree-lined parade ground patrolled periodically by warders.

Having finished breakfast, we went to put our slops into a couple of dustbins on our side of the grounds. At the same time about fifty to a hundred inmates were being escorted by warders across the parade ground. When they saw us throwing scraps into the bins, they just went berserk, broke free from their escorts and tried to swarm over; a few did make it only to be restrained by some squaddies and then batoned by warders desperately trying to restore order. Poor souls, they were some of the true victims of war, starving as their meagre rations had withered away in the months after the invasion. Several of us could not take it. I personally remembered the gnawing emptiness of childhood poverty. I asked a couple of squaddies to help me get the bins near the gate where the corporal with the key agreed to open it. The bins were transferred and as orderly as possible, the warders lined the patients up to dip into the slops. In the meantime, thank God, word had reached the kitchens about their plight and bread and other consumables were brought out and issued. The whole episode is one I would rather forget.

Capt Smart – the only man I knew on my return to the "Royal Norfolks".

We later spent many hours testing our weapons and getting ready to move to forward positions along the River Maas. I finished up in a place called Wanssum. I was allocated officially to a platoon but only saw one familiar face from my training days, a Captain Smart. We took up positions along the Maas throughout the long, bitter winter of 1944. Christmas came and went with some cheer but not the glow of a Hollywood re-enactment. The weather was unbelievable; even our weapons froze up from time to time. Eventually, on 17 December news leaked through about the 'Battle of the Bulge'. We were already fully stretched but now had to be even more on our toes. It is difficult to sum up how nerve-wracking it all was as rumours flew round that we were in for another Dunkirk as the Gerries seemed to take all before them. Initially the appalling weather had helped the German cause, but by January 1945 it was time for serious allied counter-attacks and renewed aerial bombardment.

It was unfortunately about this time that I came under the command of a glory-hunting major with few brains that he carefully kept concealed. We had a few problems as several of our sentries had gone missing patrolling the river so it was decided to send out fighting patrols without much success. Hence when Gerry introduced a nightly routine of starting up a motor boat on the other side of the river, our commanding moron called a meeting and explained his master plan. We would pinpoint the boat, watch it day and night and then, when the moment was right, move on it. With a cocksure air, he gestured for any questions. I know I had had a good deal more experience of commando operations than him and I could not stand the thought of the mess his plan might create. Having the sense by now to phrase it in a series of polite questions, I tried to explain what I saw as Gerry's motives.

'Sir, do you think there's a danger that we might fall into a Gerry trap? Some of the blokes feel that if you listen to the boat's engine, it isn't really moving, it just ticks over. Do you think it's just a decoy and they might be up to something more important either side of it? Perhaps we could, just to be on the safe side, take each side in turn and have a look before you decide.'

He looked put out to say the least but insincerely congratulated me on my positive contribution. It was obvious he had my card marked. The next night a fifteen-man fighting patrol scoured the area to the right of the boat with no luck. The following night we tried the other side; as we were waiting, the engine started and we were taken aback to see figures seemingly walking across the river to our side. We let them come up the bank with their silouhettes clear in view. I told the officer in charge they were definitely German and that their spandau machine gun crew had the gun sticking out against the night sky ready for action. We had to move quickly and with surprising efficiency we took all eleven; seven were killed and four, including two very badly wounded, were taken prisoner. It turned out that they had set earlier in their retreat a walkway built just on the water line, primitive but effective and unspotable by air reconnaissance.

After this limited success, the glory hunter, despite his obvious dislike of me, became a thorn in my side as I turned into an unofficial sounding board for all his master plans. Sometimes these could lead to heated debates, if not full-scale arguments. I remember one about frontal attacks in daylight which appeared one of his firm favourites. I argued vehemently that they were too costly in terms of lives; it was much better, when given the chance, to infiltrate the Ger-

We occupied one of these houses to avoid the bitter cold.

man lines under cover of darkness, keeping in touch with units using a wireless and waiting till dawn when the Germans took up their positions and we would have the element of surprise. As always he said he would give this some thought. Superficially he made out he liked me but I knew he was looking for the first opportunity to knock me down. Growing up in Scotland Road gives you a smell for these characters.

Eventually we moved a few miles further down the lines and yet again took up defensive positions. By this time my section was down to five men and the weather was bloody awful, the rain incessant. We were in a forward position just looking across some fields at a couple of farmhouses and out buildings. About eight yards from our slit trenches was a large detached house, worse the wear after shelling and mortar fire. But, beggars cannot be choosers, and I decided to take a look at it to see if we could use it instead of the trenches and at least have some shelter. Two of us took a chance one night, dreading it was booby-trapped or surrounded by mines, only detected by bayonet prodding and no respecters of limbs. After a couple of visits we decided to move in, removing a wall vent and bricks to give us a good view and better line of fire.

We settled down to a happy routine and I told the others I preferred to do 'stag' or guard duty on my own at night as long as they took it in turns to wake each other ie. two hours' duty, four hours' sleep each. It was all working well; we even managed to do a bit of haute cuisine in the cellar but all good things come to an end. One night we were paid a visit by our glory hunter. I heard him come in and it was obvious something had gone wrong from the mumbled conversation he was having. By this point I had had as much as I could take of this character and, God knows why, but out of sheer devilment I took out my Sten gun, put in under my greatcoat which was doubling as a blanket and pretended to be asleep. He came in and like a man who has found a million dollars, sat astride my chest and stuck his .45 revolver to my forehead. A torrent of abuse ensued. He was in the right in that one of the others had gone to sleep and the Germans could have made easy meat of us. 'I feel like blowing your bloody brains out!' He finally hissed in his moment of victory. There was just me and him in the silent cellar.

'Listen pal, you've been after me for a long while; I'm telling you now—if you don't get off my bleedin' chest, you'll have twenty-eight bullets up your arse and maybe lose the few brains you've got!' In a state of shock, he jumped up and yelled that I would be courtmartialled.

'Thank God,' I shouted back, 'Maybe I'll finally get some rest, a change of clothes and a good night's sleep!' Then two of the section came in with a sergeant and in cold resentment the remainder of the night's watch was organised. The next day I was instructed to report to headquarters, five hundred yards back, and I got the usual dressing down from the colonel. After the lecture on regulations in the British army since Caesar, I was asked if I had anything to say. 'Well, are you charging me?' I arrogantly inquired. Even the colonel seemed to have some doubt about this and I was asked to leave the room while they discussed it. On recall, I was informed that

Officers carrying 303 rifles as a ploy to fool German snipers, who usually picked officers out because of the revolvers they carried.

the issue would be held in abeyance until we came out of the line. 'I'd rather be tried now,' I interrupted, knowing full well how short of men they were. Then the powers that be started to explain we were getting reinforcements very soon and maybe the pressure of the long winter was getting to me, maybe I should stay at HQ for a few days. I was very narked at all this. 'Look, I'm not "bomb happy". You either send me back to my section or put me under arrest,' I answered back.

In the end they decided to send me back. I gave my mates a right rollicking for letting me down but we stayed in the house, two off, two on, until reinforcements arrived. It was not so very long before we were all laughing about it. Eventually our reinforcements arrived and we were all withdrawn for a short rest; at last a good shower, a change of under-clothes, a shave, a sleep and letters home. There was even a chance to have a couple of drinks. We soon found out why we were allowed such luxuries. We were to finish our training on the Maas on so-called 'Buffalos' and 'Dukes', the motorised boats which we were to use to cross the Rhine should we ever reach it. We were by now about eight miles from the damned river. We also knew that the Gerries were putting up fierce resistance the nearer we got to it. On our fourth day's rest, we were told 'That's all, folks!' and we would be moving back up the line.

By now those of us with some experience knew we were going into an attack position; we would pass through another regiment and not take over their posts. I scrutinised the faces of our new naive reinforcements when this was explained. It was amazing how many initially thought it was all going to be a piece of cake, especially as the war seemed to have turned in our favour. All this changed once the first wounded appeared or Gerry obliged with a few mortar bombs. The reactions to the first fatalities were always difficult to handle. Those of us who saw ourselves as old hands tried to encourage the rookies with a show of bravado. Everyone has to go through a first

time but still the
fear gripped our
throats by virtue
of our very expe-
rience.

Eventually, on
the night of 28
February, we took
up our positions
on the starting
line, on the out-
skirts of Kerven-
heim; kick off was

Winter, 1944.

officially 9.00 a.m. on 1 March, but Gerry had already spotted
us and sent over a few mortar bombs accompanied by the odd
burst of spandau fire. This was beyond doubt the worst time,
the waiting, the terrified anticipation. I surveyed the area we
had been allocated. It had all the ingredients of a suicide
mission; on the right about five hundred yards away was a
church, its roof already ablaze and close by a farmhouse with
some outbuildings and a couple of trees. They were all surrounded by the dreaded open country, fields with no cover.
Finally about one hundred and fifty yards to the left of the
church was a hedgerow running down to our positions. I was
by now obsessed with the dangers of hedges concealing German
troops and the outbuildings, their tanks, their mastery of
camouflage which had already earned my admiration. We for
our part had no armour to back us up nor would we until we
had completed our orders. I had a healthy respect for the
accuracy of German 88 mm guns and the fearlessness of Tiger
tank crews.

Finally the orders came. Our company, 'A' company, was
to take the farmhouse and so we agreed to move like lightning
across the open country—well, there was not any real alter-
native. I took a good old Bren gen. Then the shelling started
at 9.15 a.m. Our side thought they were doing us a good turn

by laying on a creeping barrage. I always thought they were waste of time, all they seemed to do was tell Gerry you were on your way. In we went; for the first two hundred yards we were greeted only by the occasional burst of machine gun fire. Then all hell broke out; having coaxed us to a point of no return, Gerry threw all he had at us, mortar bombs, small arms fire and everything. I had never seen carnage like it; they seemed to be everywhere as the farmhouse windows spat with machine gun fire. The friends I had made over the winter were just cut to ribbons and over one hundred lay dead or wounded within a few mind-blowing minutes. Suddenly I spotted two Gerries with a spandau in a trench by one of the trees,

Local cemetery on the outskirts of Kervenheim, where many comrades are buried. Local Germans tend the grave.

there was nothing for it. I ran towards them firing the Bren gun. One jumped up and ran to the back of the farmhouse. As the magazine on the Bren ran out, I had no choice but to jump into his trench, luckily finding his mate dead. Quickly I changed the magazine and surveyed the nightmare from the top of the trench. The Germans continued to spray the field with gunfire as the wounded groaned in terrible pain. I aimed the Bren at the farmhouse but only a single bullet fired; the damned thing had jammed on a single shot or 'repetition'. I could not get it to fire on automatic despite doing absolutely every procedure drummed into me during training. Even the dead Gerry had no weapon and the Germans, by now fully aware of my position, were ripping the earth around the trench with their fire. I sunk as low as I could for cover but, as I was only about fifteen yards from the farmhouse, I could not understand why they just did not lob a couple of stick grenades in my general direction. I now realised we were thoroughly beaten as our artillery began yet again to shell the farmhouse. At this point I had a welcome visitor in the form of a good friend, Corporal Cubbit. He too had come too far. 'All right, John, look's like we'll have to lay low till nightfall to stand any chance of getting out of this mess!' 'The Bren gun's playing up,' I informed him.

'Oh, there's luck—my sten gun's out of ammo!' We looked at the dead laying nearby but none that were close enough had anything of any use.

Then the shelling stopped and presumably some psychopath like the Major ordered some more of our guys to have another go; again there was carnage and finally those remaining withdrew while yet more wounded moaned in the grass.

As dusk approached neither Cubbit or I thought Gerry would let us have it our own way. We were soon proved right as a German with a very cultured English accent shouted for us to surrender. Poor old Cubbit put up his head to shout back and got a bullet right between his eyes. He dropped to the bottom of the trench and died within seconds. I scarcely had time to come to terms with this as the grenades finally arrived. Immediately I felt a sharp pain in my back and warm blood running down my shirt. Looking back, I do not know why but I took my battledress jacket off and that was the last I remember. Presumably I passed out but when I regained consciousness I found three Gerries staring down at me. Two lifted me out.

'Yer all right, I can walk on my own,' I insisted. Again the cultured accent came. An officer was one of the three. In better English than I have ever mastered he told me somewhat ominously, 'For you the war is over.'

I was taken to a barn where I was the only Brit among a load of Gerries. They were all parachute troops, experienced fighters now being used as infantry. A lot were wounded and basic first aid was being administered. I was given a cup of coffee and then a fellow dressed in a long white overall decorated with a red cross examined my back. I do not think I realised till much later how bad the wound was; it was strategically placed so I could not see the damage. He dabbed something on which looked like tissue paper and then wrapped layers of it around me. It certainly felt more secure. The officer then put me through my paces, asking from where in England I came. I told him Liverpool to which he replied that he had visited England numerous times before the war but never Liverpool. At this point one of the Gerries standing nearby came over and flicked up the safety catch on his rifle, presumably with the intention of shooting me. The officer grabbed the weapon, bawled out a lot of authoritarian orders and pushed him away. He then turned back to me and introduced me to another German. 'Get up, this is your escort. You will be taken back behind the lines and eventually you will reach your prison camp. Name and number?'

I muttered the statutory response. He then went on to say that they had searched my jacket and could find no 'flashes' on my uniform and no pay book. Indeed, they looked around my neck when I was unconscious and again found no dog tags.

Carriers continuing advance after capture of Kervenheim.

Lt Laurie leading his platoon out of Kervenheim.

He knew from the dead that we were 'A' company, the Royal Norfolks, but asked if I could explain these discrepancies. I thought on my feet and stammered I had only just joined the company from England so my uniform and everything had been issued in a rush. I tried to bluff that as I was new to all this, I presumed my particulars were placed in stores before the attack. I doubt if he was satisfied with this, but he was sufficiently happy to send me on my way. I was asked if I could walk and entrusted to my escort. He then wished me goodbye and good luck, a real gent!

9

The Long Trek

THE Gerry escort proved to be a decent guy, giving me a smoke and chatting in broken English as we trundled along. He regularly helped me to shelter as the American and Canadian air forces continually flew low and machine gunned anything that moved. Here I felt the ultimate paradox; I wanted the firing and the shelling to have the desired effect but realised I was in serious danger of being one of the allies' hits.

All kinds of crazy thoughts passed through my mind as I painfully edged along. For example, would our skirmish be reported in the daily news? I found out later it received no such mention, although the officers who fell were duly recorded individually in print. That was one elitist practice which disgusted a lot of us—the way 'other ranks' were just presented as collective numbers. We all used to say the only time an 'other rank' had his name spelled out was on his gravestone, if he was lucky! I later discovered that in the last attack five officers were killed, five wounded, thirty-six 'other ranks' were killed and one hundred and fifteen wounded; four were missing, including my good self. (The killed were all buried locally and I have returned to the cemetery on holidays abroad to pay my respects. The area is very well kept by local Germans).

Much to my annoyance I also found out later that two nights after the carnage of 1 March, the tactics we had discussed relating to night infiltration were successfully employed and the Gerries, totally surprised to find themselves surrounded, surrendered quietly with no loss of life.

Anyway, back to my stroll through Germany! I did my best
to go slowly, hoping for an opportunity to slip the net. All
this seemed extremely unlikely given that I was surrounded
by dozens of Germans. I was shocked by how badly equipped
the enemy were; in a journey lasting some eight miles, I counted
only twenty-five lorries and five tanks, two of which, according
to my escort, had no petrol. The roads seemed crowded with
pathetic horse-drawn carts and even handcarts. Sadly after a
couple of miles my 'soft touch' escort handed me over to
another, far sterner guard, older, wiser and far more shrewd.
His name sounded something like Herbie; well, he got that
from me during our time together. He immediately insisted I
walk faster, to escape the shelling. His English was good, his
militaristic, 'by the book' attitude depressing. He insisted we
avoided town and village centres, again mainly because of the
bombing, the mere mention of which embittered his mood.
To be fair, the devastation, indeed the sheer desolation, had
to be seen to be believed. Images of mile upon mile of rubble
and dust are imprinted upon my mind. Herbie also said it
would be safer for me as British troops were not exactly flavour
of the month locally. We walked for three days and nights; in
retrospect, I cannot imagine how my injury allowed for this.
Sometimes Herbie would stop for rations, usually at army field
kitchens where we were issued with hard brown bread, stale
cheese and hot coffee. Sometimes he had to approach private
houses. On one such occasion, he ordered me to stay at the
gate as he knocked. The housewife duly supplied him with
coffee and sandwiches but got pretty rattled when she spotted
me. I spoke only a smattering of German but managed to grasp
the repetitive shrillness of 'Kien essen für Engländer!'

Herbie quickly came over to me, gave me a verbal dressing
down and ordered me to move on, all a show to satiate her
anger. After that, his attitude seemed to soften and he even
became more talkative and protective as the bombing continued
unabated. I think he did not know what to do for the best;
whenever we stopped for a rest he always kept his gun ready

in case I tried anything, yet he knew the war was coming to an end and most German troops were anxious to surrender to the British or the Yanks rather than the Russians. My own heart sank as we reached the Rhine. Once across I felt my chances of escape were gone. As we approached the river, the congestion was unbelievable; troops, horses and carts were easy picking for fighter pilots as the buildings along the banks burned in ruins.

We reported to a soldier wearing a metal chain with a medallion around his neck who appeared to be in charge of the chaos as some kind of shoremaster. By now it was dusk; our papers were inspected and we then moved up to the water's edge towards what I thought was a jetty. On closer inspection, it proved to an enormous raft made out of wooden planks and forty-five gallon steel drums. How it all fitted together was beyond me. Not only were we packed on board but at least another four horse and carts and as many troops as the shoremaster could muster. Herbie and I ended up in the centre between two carts where he kept insisting I kept close to him; God knows where he thought I was going to go! The carts were being clamped by steel rings to the raft as I saw soldiers removing a large camouflage net along the bank to reveal a battered tug boat which was quickly coupled to our landing stage. Herbie told me to hold on tight to a cart as we took off as the crossing could be rough. I heard a couple of splashes but was too exhausted to care as long as it was not me. Herbie confided that this type of manoeuvre was being repeated under cover of darkness at several points up and down the river.

As we reached the other side, more splashes were heard and once moored, the long trek recommenced. I noticed signs for Duisburg and Dusseldorf as the constant drone of aircraft and blasts of heavy bombing became incidental background noise. Herbie said we were heading for Dusseldorf and further orders; we thus arrived about midday at a compound for displaced persons. The city itself was just one mass bomb site. As far as the eye could see, there was not one undamaged building. The Germans, however, literally living in the rubble, were going about their business with an air of resigned normality. By this point on my walk I started to doubt allied propaganda about the effect of bombing on German civilian morale; if anything, it seemed to make them more determined to adjust to the demands of war.

The displaced persons camp was next to some railway marshalling yards. It comprised about ten to fifteen huts, ten foot wide, thirty foot long, surrounded by wire and guard posts and manned by what can only be described as geriatric soldiers. These proved to be literally right old bastards, vindictive and cruel. Herbie left me with one who took me to a hut and pushed me into a dark narrow passage two foot wide which ran the full length of the building. On the left I could make out what I can only describe as shelves, about two foot apart from floor to ceiling and about eight foot deep. I could feel the dank stench of humanity around me and, as my eyes adjusted to the limited light, I could see pathetic bundles of people sleeping on these shelves.

'Any English?' I choked. The replies indicated every European nationality, even a few Asians, but no British. I wryly understood a comment I had once heard about being lonely in a crowded room. Some of my room mates were in a dreadful condition, lousy with dirt, little clothing and most had no boots or shoes, just rags. Herbie's parting words of 'keep on your boots' now made sense. All were weak and thin. It slowly dawned on me that I was on the same rapid downhill slope; my wound and belly ached, I had not shaved or washed in a week and my only clothes were the shirt and trousers I stood in plus the belt which I still have to this day. I always thought it was the horse shoe buckle which got me through.

After what seemed like hours, it was about 5.00 p.m., and one of the old bastards plus a Gerry soldier arrived with more DPs. The soldier told me I would be staying a while and pushed me aggressively towards a heap of rubbish outside the door. In very good English he snapped, 'Find yourself a tin can and you can have some soup.' Without dignity I scrabbled through the garbage; there was not one can to be had. The old bastard was then told to fetch me one; I swear he brought back the rustiest he could find. I was then dragged to a shed where said can was filled with what was, as far as I was concerned, grass and tepid water; a three-inch chunk of bread was also shoved at me. The old bastard rifle-prodded me back to the hut where the other DPs looked on ravenously as I had my tea. Warily I found a spot on a shelf near the door and consumed my 'cuisine'. I then spent an uneasy night listening to the incessant bombing and explosions and praying for Herbie's return.

Daylight had never been more welcome and at dawn we were all ordered out of the hut which by now smelt like an open sewer. The experienced DPs dashed off to the shed for breakfast, lining up excitedly for yet more grass soup and rye; the newer inmates including myself brought up the rear. Most were then frogmarched off to work clearing up the debris from the night before. I was shepherded back to the hut. Herbie arrived and off we went. I noticed the DP huts had POW markings and commented maybe that was why they were not bombed.

Herbie looked at me in exasperation, 'The camp has been bombed many, many times,' he muttered monotonously. I still tried to be pleasant as I was genuinely pleased to see him. 'God, it's good to talk English to you. No one in that hut was English. No one understood me. Can you credit it! Not one!' I said as I saw the flicker of a smile on his face. In my bravado I half hoped I would gain his confidence, catch him unawares, disarm him and make my escape. Slowly it dawned on my tired, rattled brain that I perhaps could have managed it a few days earlier but with each passing hour I grew perceptibly weaker and downright sick. Finally I realised the futility of my position as we trudged through the wreckage of Dusseldorf.

Needless to say, after half an hour, the sirens wailed and hundreds of Yankee Flying Fortresses made their appearance.

With similar predictability the German ack-ack guns started and Herbie decided we were taking too many chances and withdrew to relative safety until the worst had passed. As we sat in a crowded public shelter for over an hour, the explosions were some of the loudest I had ever heard. As we came back up into the daylight, there, in the middle of some smoking rubble was a Flying Fortress; one wing had gone but the fuselage was still intact. We stood about five hundred yards away as a crowd moved in towards the wreckage and a couple of men climbed inside. Two air force men were lifted out and thrown on the debris and then a final third. The mob leaders produced some long-handled spades and literally hacked at the bodies. My stomach lurched as I prayed they were already dead. Bystanders were then invited to take turns apiece; most participated with lusty relish as blood sprayed their ragged clothing. Close to nausea, I looked at Herbie. 'Not good, let's go quick.'

Eventually Dusseldorf was behind us and we walked through open country. I started to badger Herbie about my appearance.

'Look, pal, any chance of a wash? A shave?' I asked and gesticulated repeatedly. He never answered as we came to a wood crawling with Gerries, at last behaving with the sort of military antics Will Hay had led me to expect. They all appeared remarkably well equipped as we passed through a barrier into some kind of camp. To one side I noticed hundreds of gas cylinders stacked up army-style.

'What's all that for?' I whispered as several eyes bore into us.

'Gas. We may have to use it soon,' Herbie muttered, embarrassed and totally on edge.

God, I thought, they must be getting desperate. We then entered what looked like a large air raid shelter but inside I could hear engines revving permanently, generators supplying electricity. We went underground to what appeared to be the stores where I was given two parcels wrapped in thick tin foil, two round white boxes and a packet of powder. They turned out to be bread, cheese and coffee. 'Twenty years old,' Herbie confided.

The bread tasted like liquorice and the cheese smelt like it was evolving but by now anything was good to me. As a tea connoisseur I could not really rate the coffee!

'This is all we get now till the prison camp. Make it last,' Herbie warned as he led me back to daylight and deposited me in a huge outbuilding while he went to get his orders. While chewing on my rations I glanced around me; it seemed to be a huge kitchen of some description, well, there was a whole wall of ovens and the place felt pretty warm and recently used. The atmosphere was weird as apart from the ovens, the room was starkly empty. With the benefit of hindsight, in later life I shudder to think what the real purpose of the camp was but the gas, the ovens and the tight security point to only one conclusion.

Herbie, thankfully, soon returned, explaining it was on to Cologne and our final instructions. He said quite openly that he was worried about taking me any further after the incident with the Flying Fortress. 'You must try to look very sick.' I said he must be joking as I really was feeling lousy. I tried to stress that my dressing has never been changed, I felt on fire and could not walk much further. As I had not moaned before, he went quiet and quickly changed the subject. Off to Cologne we trotted.

Cologne was a peculiar sight; one majestic, bomb-blasted cathedral rising out of miles of dereliction. Six Tiger tanks guarded the entrance and Herbie hurriedly explained that there had been some looting and these were necessary to discourage unauthorised personnel entering the building; indeed there were orders to shoot on sight. The looting story turned out to be a con; we had to go inside for Herbie's orders and then it was a plain as the nose on your face that Gerry was using the place as a command centre. The place was abuzz with officers issuing orders as civilians and military personnel speedily went about their duties. All the Germans were armed and

it was soon obvious that I was not flavour of the month. I
stuck close to Herbie as the American bombing recommenced.
Some of the Gerries began to make very nasty gestures in my
general direction as Herbie rapidly picked up his orders and
shuffled me out of the building and the city.

Our next destination, it appeared, was to be Koblenz, but
we would have a bit of a walk before we could catch a train.
I was by now on the verge of collapse; exhaustion numbed
pain. Herbie reluctantly agreed to try to cadge a lift and soon
cajoled, well threatened, a passing horse and cart driver to let
us on board.

'You are an important prisoner. I must deliver you to
Koblenz. I will be punished severely if I do not deliver you.
Do not try to escape,' Herbie warned as he helped me on to
the cart.

His words at first bemused and then worried me. Why was
I so important? I eventually dismissed his words as an attempt
to make me behave myself. Fairly soon afterwards we boarded
a train and I was a bit put out when I was shoved into a
cattle-truck with one other soul. Herbie went off with another
soldier to a guard's van which doubled as a canteen for the
Gerries.

The cattle-truck was bolted from the outside and as the
train pulled out, my companion scrabbled over to my corner;
he was dressed in 'civvies' which had seen better days, his
shoes were odd, made out of some plastic material. He later
gesticulated that he had made them himself. He wore no socks
but in a variety of gestures made it clear how much he admired
my filthy boots. Making himself comfortable beside me, he
then produced a small tin from his pocket and started to roll
a cigarette; the paper was newsprint, the tobacco some kind
of straw. Out of a second tin lined with an oily rag, he produce
a needle and piece of flint stone; he struck one with the other
to make the spark necessary to light the oily rag. From its
smoulderings he lit his ciggy; after a couple of puffs he offered
me some which I graciously declined. He kept pointing to

himself and chattering, 'Rooskie!, Rooskie!' So he was Russian, so I replied, 'Englander', which he smilingly repronounced. I nodded, we shook hands and spent the rest of our journey trying to explain our backgrounds with no small amount of comedy. After what seemed like a couple of hours the train slowed down and the door was thrown back to reveal the countryside. Herbie and another Gerry ordered me down. Stiff with pain I stumbled, helped almost tenderly by the Russian. I turned to thank him only to see him being rifle-butted to the ground as his guard bolted the truck. I was instantly enraged but was dragged off by Herbie who, with uncharacteristic sensitivity, repeatedly apologised for the incident.

We then trundled along the Rhine and I had my first chance to appreciate, despite the circumstances, the magnificent castles. Herbie singled one out as our destination. 'You will stay there for a while to rest,' he confided, 'rest' from my point of view seemed to have ominous overtones.

As we approached the schloss the inevitable bombing started but for once Herbie was oblivious to shelter, telling me to get

a move on as we only had half an hour to go. It was obvious that whatever had been said to him in Cologne or perhaps even on the train made him want me off his hands as quickly as possible. We finally entered a huge courtyard via a gate where a very smart guard inspected our papers in true Prussian style and with a cavalier disdain of the bombing. Hurriedly, almost brusquely, Herbie bade me farewell; as he scuttled off into history I felt I had lost my final protector. As I was marched across the yard, my only recollection was of a metal-roofed traffic island surrounded by sand bags. It was a sentry post and inside were two Gerries and a couple of spandau machine guns aimed permanently at incoming and outgoing traffic. I was taken to an office occupied by a very smooth looking officer and two soldiers. I was invited to sit on a chair.

'We are very sorry you have had such a rough journey, inevitable in the circumstances but now you will have a good rest,' he said with a sardonic smile, his English worthy of the BBC. This guy was definitely up to something; he then asked for my particulars.

'By the way, have you found your dog tags and pay book?' I gestured no and he immediately rapped the desk and yelled in German. Two soldiers then bounced into the room and dragged me out. Both had large torches strapped to their chests which proved essential as we rushed down some stone steps into the bowels of the castle. It was dark, coldly damp as water dripped all over the ceilings. We passed down a narrow corridor lined on one side with thick doors. One was opened and in I was pushed; someone yelled I would get breakfast the next day.

Time seemed momentarily to stand still; as I tried to readjust to the pitch black cell, I calculated it was about 6.00 p.m. Literally everything was black and wet; water dripped in unending blackness. I felt the walls and tried to count my steps in an attempt to put size to void. It was about nine steps square; the walls and floor appeared to be of solid granite and the cold was invasive. I tried to keep walking to occupy mind and body; sitting on the wet floor did not appeal, if my Mam had been here she would have warned me against piles!

After an eternity a guard shouted in English to get away from the door. In my custodial blindness, I rushed out to find the door; it opened and breakfast was served followed by the slam of darkness. On all fours my hands slowly felt out for the precious rations; despite my efforts, I knocked over the tin can, spilling its contents. With little human dignity I licked the rough granite; it had been coffee. I felt for and found the ubiquitous three-inch chunk of stale bread, by now wet and soggy. I then tried to supplement my water supply by sitting with my mouth open catching the odd droplets. It provided mental and physical recreation as I kept count of my successes. I edged near the door, straining to hear any sound. All that came through was a muted rumbling, presumably the bombing. I could feel what was left of my strength draining into the damp. I felt hot and the wound was making its presence known. I finally reached a stage where I did not know if I was standing, sitting or lying down. The blackness absorbed me.

As it turned out, I received another four breakfasts but in what was left of my consciousness, I thought they were lunch, tea and supper. Time had no meaning until the fifth day when suddenly and without warning the cell door flew open. I sat motionless, brain stem dead. They dragged me out but, to be fair, they helped me up the stone steps. Daylight hit my eyes; it was an awful feeling. Sick, disorientated, confused, I was sat on a wooden bench for about an hour. Slowly, painfully, I came round. As my eyes started to focus, I could make out the sandbagged gun post, the Gerries inside. My brain began to function in very low gear. It was at this point I caught a glimpse of an English officer, a lieutenant; his shoulder flashes were either KSLE or DCLI, my eyes were not that trustworthy. He glanced back at me sympathetically as the guards hurried him across the yard, shoved him through one of the wooden doors and then raced back to the machine gun post. With almost theatrical speed, they put two bursts into the door, some fifty plus bullets. 'You bastards!' I thought but the action served to trigger me back to life. I later found out it was just a trick and the guy was pulled clear before they fired. They had wanted to scare me but my anger had the reverse effect.

I was then taken back to the officer I had met on arrival. In a sarcastically sycophantic tone he inquired about my health. 'Well, John, did you enjoy your five days of rest? Feeling refreshed?'

I thought, 'You're some smooth bastard, I'll play you at your own game.' Summoning up as much of a Noel Coward approach as I could muster, I replied, 'Oh, the facilities were all right but I would recommend a few optional extras, like a wash, shave, light, bed, perhaps even a book to read. After all, even in the worst English hotel there's always a Bible.'

He looked suitably annoyed and I had the feeling I would pay for this. He played with a Red Cross parcel on his desk and stated all I had to do was to answer a few questions and my requests would be granted. I could even have the parcel and the food and cigarettes it contained. I replied that I was feeling pretty rough and would it be possible to see a doctor before we started. At this point he went mad, jumping to his feet screaming, 'I will ask the questions, not you!'

He yelled a tirade of abuse, the guards present looked uncomfortably tense. He then proceeded to ask me all kinds of erroneous questions about my army career; he already knew the answers to the few relevant queries. For sheer bloody-mindedness, feeling there was nothing left to lose, at first I told him the opposite of what he expected to hear. He then confirmed he knew about the First Battalion, the Royal Norfolks, mentioning some of the officers I knew. A phone call interrupted this nonsense and then silence. Finally we came back to the dog tags.

'Where is your pay book? When did you last have it? Where are your dog tags? When did you last see them? What is your father's surname? When did you fly to Germany, in what type of plane?'

I stuck to my story about being a late reinforcement, hence the lack of pay book and flashes, 'My uniform was brand new; there was no time! Look at the state it's in now, thanks to you lot!' I pointed to the filthy rags I wore. This insult to the Reich induced another fit of recriminations which were brought to an abrupt end as the door sprang open. Everyone jumped to attention as in walked the smartest looking German officer I had ever seen. He was almost majestic in his dark blue uniform bedecked in all kinds of silver braid. He had a couple of rows of medal ribbons and there between his jacket glinted the Iron Cross. He was tall, over six foot and although not handsome, imposing and distinguished. He was greying at the temples and had a couple of scars on his face that looked like shrapnel wounds. On one of his sleeves, about five inches above his wrist was the word 'Leibstandarte'. At the time it meant nothing but I made a mental note and later found out it signified that the guy must have belonged at one time to Hitler's personal guard. Automatically, without thinking, I saluted him. He acknowledged my salute and spoke for a while in German to my interrogator. Another smart officer entered and said to me in excellent English, 'We are going for a walk now in the castle grounds.' He took my arm and led me outside. 'My commanding officer will be joining us shortly; he wants to have a quiet word with you. I will follow closely to protect him.'

'From who?' I asked in all sincerity. 'You, of course, just in case you get any heroic ideas.'

'Oh come off it, it's taking me all my time just to stand up and walk. I'm wounded in case you haven't noticed. Anyway he looks as though he can look after himself,' I muttered dejectedly as the senior officer arrived.

'Come, here, we will sit and rest.' He pointed to a bench. I sat down looking out at the Rhine, almost daydreaming. 'Now, John, you must appreciate that I am not interrogating you. I wanted a chat for my own personal interest. I am anxious to understand the English, especially those from ordinary work ing backgrounds. In some countries one only hears of things from the aristocracy's point of view. So, John, are you interested in politics? Do you have political sympathies?'

I was evasive, knowing full well he would try to exploit any disaffection I might imply. 'Yes, I have my own political opinions but I think the army's right when you're told to set aside differences during a war.' Obviously I had given the game away that I was none too happy with the status quo circa 1939 as straightaway he asked, 'So, what do you think of your Mr Churchill?'

'A good leader for wartime.' I replied

'What do you mean by that?' He almost seemed interested.

'Well he's yet to prove himself as a peacetime P.M.' I added.

'So, perhaps Mr Churchill's earlier time in office did not give him enough of the right sort of reputation?' He stated rhetorically. I shrugged, pretending not to understand though I had heard enough propaganda on Scottie Road about the guy and his tactics, in Ireland, against Welsh miners as well as Gallipoli to know what was being implied.

'And your childhood in England, John, was it good? Your schooling, for instance? Did you join any clubs?'

'I had a fine time. The teachers did their best, I suppose. I only went to elementary school. I can't remember if there were formal clubs to join. I was probably too busy kicking a football.'

'Ah, sport, yes. War is like sport, is it not? The men on both teams respect each other; this is very true of combat troops, don't you agree?' Without waiting for an answer, he continued, 'We in Germany are always sad that England is not our ally in our struggle. As people we have so much in common, in our standards, our culture. To be at war with England is something I personally regret.' This was said with an air of truthfulness.

'Yes, but if we'd had supported you, would we have been equals or underdogs?' He examined his hands evasively as I stared ahead at the Rhine.

'As you may be aware, John, I am a member of the SS. We have many nationalities in our movement, Dutch and French for example, carefully selected from prisoners of war like yourself. Obviously they have volunteered to join us and we have vetted them. They, I can assure you, are our equals, those who share our dream.'

He looked at me full face, regretfully as if he sensed it was a dream I would never share or perhaps a dream that had already become a futile, failed nightmare. I felt that in many ways the interview was over, but as the spring sun glinted on the water, he began to talk about England in general. He asked where I was from but, I think, had already guessed. He knew Southport well. He had spent the whole of 1937 there and he reminisced about his seaside haunts with a tinge of sadness.

'Well, I must bow to your superior knowledge. Never been there myself; I don't think they encourage day trips by lads from Scotland Road,' I commented. I do not know if he understood my sentence literally but he laughed good-naturedly as if he took my meaning.

'Now, John, thank you for our chat.' Glancing at his watch he added, 'Before I send you on, do you have any requests?'

'Could I see a doctor? This thing's killing me and it had not been looked at for nearly a week. Oh, any chance of a wash?'

'Yes, I think we can see to all that,' he replied, and stood up as we walked back to the castle. Sure enough, I was then taken to a medical room where it was sheer bliss to have a swill down and clean dressings. I was even given a decent cup of coffee and a reasonable piece of cheese. Thus restored, I was taken back to my benefactor and I thanked him perhaps too heartily for an enemy. He informed me that I was being taken to Limburg on Mainz and then to Stalag 12A, Wetzlar, my POW camp. Transport was being organised. I again thanked him with a sense of relief as I at last knew something of my fate. He bade me goodbye and good luck and I think I amused him as I saluted him with a respect bordering on deference. He smiled and left.

So that afternoon I, three other prisoners and four guards set off for Stalag 12A. Transport proved to be a horse and cart but nevertheless it was much appreciated. It was sheer luxury; in between the air raids I was even able to take a nap; even the spring weather was welcome after five days in solitary. At Limburg we changed carts after more interminable documentation and trudged inexorably into Wetzlar.

10

My First Holiday Camp

A S WE were processed by the camp authorities I took in as much as I could. There were quite a few Gerry guards, lots of huts, dogs, machine gun posts and barbed wire. There was an eerie absence of POWs. Eventually we were led through the camp to the English compound, a single solitary hut; I later discovered that most of the prisoners were Russians although there were also some Yanks. One guard opened the door of our future home. The stench was terrible—overwhelming, nauseating. Another guard jumped inside to speak to one of the prisoners and then the four of us were shoved through the door which, as ever, was slammed decisively and locked.

Within seconds we were surrounded by RAF types, well-spoken flying officers, most of whom, as it turned out, were not English but from what is now called the white Commonwealth: Canada, Australia, South Africa and New Zealand; indeed, as far as the UK went, there was me as the only Englishman and two Welsh guys. The majority were Canadian. For what seemed like hours we were interrogated by the assembled company; in some ways it was more gruelling than anything I had previously experienced. A makeshift map was dragged out as they excitedly asked us to plot our positions. Our news seemed to give them great heart; from their perspective the Allies now had Gerry firmly on the run.

I meticulously took in my new surroundings; there were forty-one of us in a hut twelve metres by nine. There were rickety double-tier wooden bunks filled with loose, filthy straw.

Most of us were wounded, some quite badly. Infection invaded the very air; it was only a matter of time before all shared the endemic dysentery. There were absolutely no washing facilities and the only 'toilet' as such was a forty-five gallon steel drum; this was emptied daily into an odious cesspit outside the inner compound by the so-called 'fitter' among us; even suffering and sickness are relative.

With the interrogation over, a Canadian briefed us on all these arrangements. He was obviously the hut leader, one Frank Anderson, a Clark Gable look-alike with a keen sense of humour who earned and deserved our respect. He issued us with our tin cans which he partially filled with water. 'Make the most of this, guys, we won't get any more till tomorrow morning. Guard the cans like your household silver. In here they are probably worth more. And, look here our luxury item, the communal razor blade. We'll set aside a little water tomorrow so you can have a wash and shave.'

Despite the atrocious conditions, it was really good to be back among friendly faces. Some of the chaps were in a terrible state, their wounds having been allowed to fester for some time, but it was frightening how quickly we all adjusted to the monotonous routine of camp suffering as the weeks passed. We were only let out of the hut once a day to be counted while the toilet drum was emptied. The whole procedure would

M-Stammlager XII A

№ 050776

P.o.w. number and Stalag.

take about fifteen minutes but we would always endeavour to make it last longer for a few more precious minutes in the fresh air. It became our daily game, our daily ritual as we slowly dragged the wounded in and out. Once back in the hut, there you stayed, all on the verge of going 'stir crazy', unless Gerry did us the honour of a spot check. The main highlight of the day was obviously the daily food ration. Forty-one slices of bread, half an inch thick, three inches square, one two gallon pail of 'soup' or salty potato water, one two gallon pail of drinking water. Frank distributed the rations fairly; given the Darwinian desire, the atmosphere at dinner time could be pretty tense.

Our only regular visitor was a Gerry sergeant, Klaus Pinnow. We all liked him despite the circumstances. He was an ordinary bloke, a good guy, an ex-combat soldier who had been wounded many times. He was from Breslau and had fought on the eastern front with some distinction. He loathed the Russians, claiming they were lower than animals. He had also fought in Crete and against the 8th Army in the desert; his admiration for the British was genuine. Now deemed unfit for active service, he was lumbered with stalag life and hated every minute of it. It disgusted him and we all knew it. Sometimes on his rounds he would drop a couple of potatoes or turnips in a bunk as he passed. He always had a lot of dog ends, cigars as well as cigs, which were ironically a life line for the badly wounded.

We also shared our wretched conditions with untold thousands of vermin; everyone's head was alive with lice and we all lived and slept in the clothes in which we had been captured. The straw in the bunks had a life of its own; it was never changed. Circumstances soon took their toll; dysentery and diet produced staggering weight loss even among those who had started their imprisonment relatively fit. Too many of the chaps were getting to the stage where they could no longer walk. Sleep was problematic; time crept by with painful slowness. We honestly tried to make the best of it and took it in turns to raise spirits collectively and individually. We spent hours reliving our past lives, swapping stories, and speculating on the progress of the war. Sing songs always helped; if I reached a suicidal low I would remind myself and others that there were plenty in the cemetery or dead on the battlefield who would love to be in our position. We knew them. We had seen them.

Given my health and the monotony of the incarceration it is difficult to recall too many specific incidents but I do vividly remember the day an officer paid us a visit. Klaus brought him round on his usual house call chatting away in German. As they went to leave some soft sod shouted at the top of his voice, 'You German bastard!'

Deathly silence and the ructions ensued. The officer screamed a torrent in German and then in 'Yankee English' demanded to know who had dared to insult him. Again silence. The officer stormed out. Klaus scurried behind him, quickly locking the door. About two hours later Klaus returned and pleaded for the man to come forward; he then informed us that the guards would soon be coming to take eight men away for punishment unless the culprit came forward. He looked scared and said we had one hour to consider the offer. In the end we went along with Frank's advice, to pick out the eight in the worst condition. We all knew why; we thought it unlikely they would survive whatever happened. Four guards duly arrived and, as one of the eight, I left the compound a very worried man. We were taken about five hundred yards to a small hut; inside in the middle of the room there were two long wooden benches, about a yard apart. In two of the corners there were two guards, each with a machine gun. Four of us were put on one bench, four on the other. It is an understatement to say our blood ran cold. We were ordered to face each other and remain silent. After ten minutes of eternity the door sprang open and in bounced two Gerries with a folding table and brief cases. They set up their equipment, opened the cases and produced two open cut throat razors. They then hung strops on the window catches and started sharpening the razors with meticulous rhythm. We stared sideways in horror; we had earlier discussed some of the rumours we had heard about German atrocities and I remembered vividly the camp I had visited on my way to Koblenz. After several minutes the officer in charge issued his orders and one of the 'cut throat' guys headed towards me. I then got the surprise of the war—he started to cut my hair with scissors and then shaved my head. I found it difficult despite the discomfort to control my delight. Goodbye lice! Unfortunately I think the officer saw my reaction. New orders were barked and from then on the others had only half a head shaved, the front, back or side. One poor chap lost half his pride and joy, his handlebar moustache, symbol of his pre-prison vanity and lady-conquering days. By this point the Gerries were laughing, to be fair good-naturedly not only at our comic appearance but the stupidity of the whole task. We too relaxed and saw the funny side. Back at the hut we later re-enacted the whole scene like a pantomime. It bucked us up for days; something had actually happened!

I was taken prisoner on 1st March and must have arrived at Wetzlar about a week or so later. I became institutionalized rapidly to POW life. In later years I could never watch films about prison camps without disbelief, occasional anger and ironic amusement; the thought of putting on plays, exercising with a wooden horse, being invited to take part in a football match, were all beyond my comprehension. My reality would probably have been too strong for the stomachs of movie-goers in the fifties.

11

The beginning of the end

THE MONOTONY of camp ritual came to an unexpected, indeed dramatic end in the pitch dark of the night of 24 April. I was never sure of the exact time but in what seemed like the middle of the night, we were roused by the guards screeching 'Raus, raus!' and telling us to be ready to move in half an hour. Our bewilderment was immeasurable. We were then lined up outside the hut and counted; we were ordered to march, but wounds, diet and dysentery had taken their toll and some of us could hardly stand. We were thus dragged along by healthier comrades as the nervous Germans incessantly prodded and jostled us. This seemed to go on for about a mile; all the time we could hear Wetzlar being bombed. In a state of near panic the guards herded us into a railway siding and shoved us into a waiting cattle truck, all forty-one of us, with no toilets, no edible rations. We were to rot in this box for several days.

After our initial shock died down we noticed two small openings, about twelve inches by nine covered with barbed wire at each end of the truck. We would later take it in turns to draw fresh air from these. We quickly tried to improvise lavatory arrangements by unsuccessfully trying to lever up some of the floor; in more ways than one dysentery is a mover of men. In the end we had to use one corner of the truck; there was no other solution.

Thus our last incarceration began. We seemed to be there for over two days listening to yet more cattle trucks being shunted to join ours; in the end there were about ten to twenty, all full of POWs, mainly Americans captured at the Battle of the Bulge. They appeared to be in an even sorrier state than us. We indulged in endless speculation about our fate, genuine exhilaration being tempered by steel cold fear of the unknown. The general consensus was that we were being taken hostage until the end of the war. Most of us silently meditated upon our eventual fate but rarely articulated our true fear of massacre.

At daybreak on the third day the train actually began to move; we shunted along for about fifteen miles and then ground to a sickening stop. From the little we could see we appeared to be on the outskirts of a small town. About one hundred yards away from us was a heavily camouflaged ammunition train, armed to the hilt with heavy duty machine guns. By this stage many of us were 'stir crazy'; we had gone without rations and some actually suggested that we might just be abandoned. We yelled our protests at the guards and heard the Yanks join in. In the subsequent shouting we learned the guards were as badly off as us but thought supplies were on their way. We also heard that several fellows had already died in the other trucks.

Then all hell broke out! We heard the rapid approach of some US Mustang fighter planes, all guns firing, strafing our train. It had no POW markings; we were sitting ducks. Someone came running alongside opening the doors as prisoners spilled out into the field. We still must have looked like a German troop train. Then an army chaplain had a brilliant idea; he shouted at us to strip to the waist and then organised most of the men into a human P, then O, then W.

'Kneel and pray with your bare backs to the sky!' he yelled as he positioned himself in the centre of the O. Miraculously the gunning stopped though two of the Mustangs continued to circle ominously. Our luck was short-lived; a low flying spotter plane appeared and swooped photographing all and sundry. The padre pleaded with the Germans not to shoot at

it but then someone overhead must have spotted the ammo'
train. It seemed like Armageddon. The fighter planes attacked,
the train was hit, scattering debris everywhere. Yet the human
POW remained totally still and did not break up until night
fell. When the action was over there was considerable human
mess; many had been wounded or killed. The Germans tried
to round us up but the dead and the badly wounded were left
where they lay.

I decided to play dead as I thought I might as well take a
chance on being killed by the Gerries or the Yanks. In the
blackness of nightfall I edged painfully across the field to a
nearby road. After what seemed like an eternity of shuffling
I crossed the open road and headed for the US lines. I just
decided to go the opposite way to the Germans. After crawling
close to the ground alongside a hedge for half a mile I accepted
my own physical state. I was just too weak to go any further.
God, however, appeared to be on my side; I came across a
natural drain next to a field. I decided to stay there and rest
as day was slowly breaking.

I did my best to camouflage myself and spent most of the
next day watching Germany retreat, horses and carts piled
high with the military equivalents of kitchen sinks. Gunfire
beat out monotonously in the background. Towards dusk I
heard more small arms fire and then Germans walking very
close to where I lay. It was obviously their rearguard falling
back towards the east. All then was deadly silent apart from
the odd tracer bullet lighting the night sky. I tried to keep
body and soul together by drinking the water in the drain and
munching on the local greenery; dandelions seemed to be
flavour of the month. I slipped into a deep sleep, blissful
unconsciousness.

I was woken late the next morning, 28th April, with a jolt;
the rumble of trucks rolled in the distance. I must have slept
until at least 9.00 a.m. I sneaked a look over the top of my
hole like a scared hedgehog. I could see nothing although the
rumbling grew. I was by then too excited and yet to petrified

to look. Eventually I worked up the guts and popped my head over the parapet.

There it was, about a mile down the road, a Sherman tank with the most beautiful, marvellous white star. I nearly jumped for joy but what to do next? Go by the book, I thought. I followed my army training to the letter, keeping perfectly still until the tank was safely alongside, unable to turn its gun at such a close distance. I sneaked another quick look; there standing head and shoulders above the turret, Tommy gun in hand, was a real life Yankee colonel.

'God, he's a sitting duck if I was a Gerry!' I rapidly thought, but how to get his attention without having my head shot off. In the end I decided to take a chance. I jumped up shouting at the top of my voice, 'English, English! Don't shoot!'

He turned round; his look registered that he had heard something; I made sure my hands were high up in the air and shouted again, staggering after him,

'English, English! Don't shoot!'

'God damn it soldier, what the hell are you doing in this sector?' he finally yelled as he scratched his brow in disbelief. I quickly explained about the ammo' train and the rest of the prisoners—'Ninety-five per cent are Yanks,' I hastily added as his questions about directions *et al.* poured forth.

'They might have made it five or six miles ahead but most are in a bloody awful state; we haven't been fed for days and a lot of the lads are pretty ill.'

'German bastards!' he muttered as he threw down some chocolate, a can of self-heating soup and some 'Lucky Strike' cigarettes. He then barked orders down his intercom, explaining the circumstances in a slang I barely understood. I was too busy consuming the food and then vomiting.

'Heh! Any tanks?'

'I've only seen some horses and carts and a bit of infantry.'

By this point the road seemed full of Yankee tanks and stag cars moving fairly smoothly in the direction of the Germans. My colonel jumped down from his tank to thank me as a jeep

he had ordered screeched to a halt, complete with stretcher
and a couple of medical orderlies. The colonel and I shook
hands as he dashed off to finish the war.

The rest of the proceedings were a bit of a blur; I was
rushed in the jeep to an American field hospital, deloused,
washed and shaved. I was then examined by a doctor, my
wounds dressed, my details taken, given a couple of injections
and then placed in a wonderfully clean bed. I even got some
milk and eggs. I nearly cried. Everyone bar me seemed concerned about my condition and the extent of my injuries. I
was like a cat with two tails; it was great to be the well cared-for
Limey.

My rest sadly only lasted half an hour. Then another
stretcher arrived and I was taken to a tent where several doctors
took it in turns to prod my back. They explained that I was
to be sedated and transferred that afternoon to a military hospital. Apparently, I needed an immediate operation as my
wounds were badly infected. I thanked them drunkenly as the
sedation took effect. I drifted in and out of consciousness. The
next time I saw the tent it was crowded with wounded and
ex-prisoners of war.

Here I came to appreciate American organisation at its best,
vehicles arriving, hospital equipment unloaded, patched-up
wounded reloaded and transferred. Again I was approached
for my details but the interviewing officer appeared to ignore
my lack of dog tags. He told me to get a good sleep but I was
too happy to give in to it. I was then taken to a liberated camp,
Stalag Luft III, I think, which was being used as a dispersal
point.

I was getting regular injections but the pain was at last
invading my consciousness; hence the timetabled sedation. The
next thing I was sure of the was the noise of plane engines
revving up and taking off. The plane I recognised straightaway,
A Dakota (D47). The wounded were being lifted on board; I
thought I would be helpful and get up and walk but I was
strapped down and given a good rollicking from an orderly. I

stumbled out an apology but he just laughed. On board a doctor examined our labels; some of the wounded got medicine, I the usual injection. I remember the take-off but not the landing. The nightmare at last seemed over.

12

Lost Days, Happy Days

THE next few weeks were lost to me and fleeting glimpses of consciousness bordered on the surreal. I came round for a while in what looked like a bathroom, all glistening white tiles and a huge window but my arms would not move. The next reawakening was worse; although I could focus more clearly I seemed to be all trussed up like a chicken in terrible pain. The one after involved fearfully bright lights; it turned out that I had woken up on the operating table awaiting my fourth dose of surgery.

My final resurrection was slow and frightening. I was yet again in the white tiled room with the window behind me. I could make out cylinders, a table, bottles and an amazing array of tubes which fed into my bed. I gradually became aware that they were fitted to me, in my back, mouth and up my nose. My arms were strapped down at my sides, my knees bent up near my chin and held there by white sheets but the real pain seemed to be in my backside. It was really sore only because of my position.

Then I saw the door; it was ajar. With a feeling of panicky isolation I tried to shout, grunt was probably nearer the truth. A nurse popped in and out and spoke German. Quickly she returned with someone in a white overall whom I assumed to be a doctor. He was very tall with a bad scar on his forehead. Again he spoke in German. My mind raced; my escape had been a dream! I lost control and tried to free myself, crying out in desperation to be told where I was.

The nurse ran out, the doctor stayed smiling benignly and straightening the bedclothes. I went berserk. Finally the nurse returned with a woman in a uniform I recognised, the Queen Alexandra nurses; she had the rank of captain and spoke in perfect English as she took the tubes from my mouth and nose.

'Now, do be quiet, you'll be all right in a minute. You've just had a bit of a fright.'

'Where the bloody hell am I?'

'94 BMH Hamburg.'

'What's that?'

'94 British Military Hospital.'

'Oh, what are the Germans doing here?'

'They're part of our staff; they are two very efficient order-lies and you've given them a fright too—a bit ungrateful given how they've looked after you.' She swilled out my mouth with some medication.

'Did you say Hamburg? How do I know you're telling the truth?' I muttered suspiciously; the shock of awaking had not improved my manners.

'Don't be so rude. Look, if you're a good boy, after the doctors have seen you, I'll let you have a couple of visitors, squaddies like yourself. At present you're in isolation because you've been quite poorly.'

'What about the war?' I quizzed.

'The war? What about it? It's over!'

'Over! Over! Who won, I mean, we won!? What's the date?'

'Which date? Look, it's August 1945 and Germany surren-dered at the beginning of May.' She replied brusquely. She had already decided she preferred me asleep.

This momentous news hit me like a brick. The conflicting emotions made rivulets into each other, coming together in a huge mountain of questions as yet unasked. The bloody war was over, relief; we had won, pride and self-righteous indulg-ence; I had been asleep since the end of April, fear, in-comprehension and a sense of loss. Florence Nightingale then toddled off officiously while the two Germans tried to reassure me with warm smiles. Florence returned with three gents; two, a Canadian major and a captain, were with the British Army Medical Corps, the third, a Gerry professor had been in charge of the hospital when the British commandeered it and had stayed on as an administrator. They all seemed quite interested in my case, asking how I felt and where I had pain.

'How long do I do this trussed up chicken impersonation?' I asked, along with several hundred general questions. The major tried to gloss over the extent of my injuries.

'Oh, it will be a few more weeks, perhaps six or so until you're allowed to lie down normally in your terms. You've been pretty bad and we'll have to take care of you. Don't try too much too soon. You need at least one or two more operations and, all being well, after that you can go into a general ward. I must stress, John, take it easy. You need one hundred per cent rest. If you continue to improve I can release your arms during the daytime in about a week. Now, now, it's not that bad; the worst is passed and you're just cursed with a few bedsores,' he spoke quietly, reassuringly, as various waves of emotion passed over my face.

After that my social life began again in short, Nightingale-supervised, spurts; a few squaddies were allowed to come in for brief chats about twice a day as long as I did not get too excited or tired. I think I broke the monotony of their convalescences as they took it in turns to recount slowly the events of the last few months from their own individual perspectives. I, as it turns out, had been a creature of mystery and speculation.

'You'd been here a while when I arrived eight weeks ago,' one of them confided.

'We all thought you were a Gerry; there's still a few here but they thought it tactful to segregate us and we were under strict instructions to leave you alone. So we thought you must have been some big fish.'

'Fancy writing home, just a short note?' Florence interjected, pen and paper at the ready. 'One of your new pals will help you if it's too much effort.'

After my last guest had left I was feeling weary beyond belief but had a go at writing home. With naive good-naturedness I decided not to tell my mother I was wounded so I made up some yarn about special duty guarding German POWs. I kept this up in later letters, indeed for a year after. I could not see much point in worrying her about my war. Hers had had its moments. Little did I realise that she had been informed in 1945 that I was missing in action but I again made up a tale to cover my tracks.

During the next few weeks life settled down into a pleasant routine; I made friends with 'Scarhead' or 'Peter' as I later affectionately nicknamed my German male nurse. Despite the history of the previous six years this guy genuinely could not do enough for me; in return he was desperate to learn English but my Scouse accent was a bit of an obstacle. On occasions another member of the medical staff would help us translate a conversation. I soon inquired how he had got the indent on his forehead: it turned out that he had once been a blacksmith and had been kicked quite seriously by an ungrateful horse. As a result he spent a long time in hospital and had become interested in nursing. Apart from my regular visitations from squaddie pals, a variety of officers took it in turns to 'debrief' me; at first I was so tired and quarrelsome with them but they seemed used to the rudeness of the injured.

'Any chance, at last, of an AB64, Part One? An ID card might be a novelty after all this time,' I immediately asked.

Their terse reply was I would get one when I was well enough; as I was still in isolation they could not see what use one would be at present. (It was only in later years that I realised how close to death I had been and conversations like this then made more sense; some of them simply did not think I had that long left).

Eventually after six and a half months in isolation I was told I was strong enough to have my final operation. I actually remember the excitement of being wheeled down to theatre: I was like a kid going to a pantomime, the first time I had consciously been outside my white tiled cell. I registered miles and miles of corridor until I reluctantly floated away.

Waking up was again like Christmas. I was lying fully stretched out, nearly flat. What joy! I only had tubes in my back! I even fantasised that the bed sores on my bum might heal *and* I was in a ward with the other wounded. Sister, or Two Gun Annie as the lads called her (she had seen service in Burma and carried, it was rumoured, a .45 revolver in her bag), arrived with tea, biscuits and strict orders for me not to get out of bed without her express permission. I even got an English newspaper and quite a few letters had at last arrived from home. She kindly offered to read them to me, but, no way, I was in action, an independent flat man! Some were over six months old and in my eagerness I was not prepared for the news of my best friend missing in action: I just knew he was dead and for the first time in my adult life I cried for an eternity. Two Gun Annie tried to soothe me, explaining the fatigue, the anaesthetic, the excitement and the shock but it was all too much and she sedated me for my own good.

The next few months flew by in their own sweet way although I was restless to be home. Within a fortnight I was

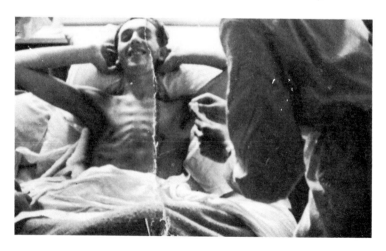

One of the best days in my life. No more operations and out of isolation into main ward.

allowed out of bed and then babied in a wheelchair. Despite Annie's advice, I sneaked off to the toilets with a couple of fellow wounded, being fed up with the very public ritual of bedpans. I had to be rescued as I felt as if my lower organs were about to fall out and was duly and rightly chastised for my disobedience. A few days later I was revisited by an army officer and actually given some ID. Then there were yet more interminable interviews with officers who at last took an interest in my lack of dog tags but who grew positively friendly as I recounted my early war. I was encouraged to walk, though it took a week or so to relearn the trick. Then, in January 1946, I was officially allowed out of bed and issued with the uniform of the walking wounded, white shirt, red tie and the worst bloody suit I have ever had in my life. These rig outs were nicknamed 'blues' by the sick who had to wear them. Basically this haute couture carried with it a host of good old army regulations; you had to be in the hospital at set times, indulge in no alcohol and, above all, you received no pay.

As it turns out, pay was not at first a problem; the currency in the real German economy at the time was cigarettes, chocolates, coffee, soap and anything edible and although there was a theoretical policy of non-fraternisation with our vanquished enemy, our local black economy was at an all-time peak. Now this was just the sort of barter society I remembered from pre-war Scotland Road and I wanted to be part of the excitement or, as I repeatedly asked the powers that be, to have a real uniform and/or be flown back to Blighty. They denied the request for the uniform; I was evidently going to have to make my own arrangements but was promised I would be on the first plane home when the quacks gave me the okay.

Mr Macawber was definitely right; something always does turn up in life and my 'something' was the squaddy in the next bed, a big Welsh fellow, a real professional soldier whom I naturally called Taffy. He had been based in Hamburg with the military police. Oh what luck! Protection, uniforms, nights out on the town, my mind raced at the possibilities!

'Any chance your pals could borrow some uniforms for us? You know, the odd trip outside?' I asked when I was sure he was restless and on the mend, trying desperately to suppress my excitement.

'Can't see why not,' he replied with a knowing smile. We planned our first excursion with more meticulousness than Operation Overlord itself. We carefully changed into our borrowed feathers in a toilet inside the hospital grounds where

Self and my military policeman friend in our blues. 94 British Military Hospital.

we hid our 'blues' for the return trip, Then it was off to see
the sights. On our first outing I was near collapse, having
walked for an hour, so we made do with a little patched café
we stumbled across. The owner politely reminded us of the
non-fraternisation rules but we patted him reassuringly and
told him we were military police. After that he could not do
enough for us so, when leaving I offered him some cigarettes.
He hesitantly, longingly refused. The poor sod thought he was
being set up. 'Oh, for Christ's sake have them,' I pushed them
cordially into his pocket as his face exploded with delight.
Needless to say we became regular welcome customers.

The return journey was smoothly uneventful. We changed
back into our medical garb and although we were late, we were
evidently not missed. After this we became bolder; some of
the others in the ward rated Lubeck above Hamburg as a
source of night life; there was even a British army club, the
'Crusader', which sold English beer. Those in the know said
it was easy to get lifts, even in 'blues', as the main route was
always crowded with army trucks and drivers ready to take
pity on fellow squaddies. We decided to have a go and the
information was sound; we had no transportation problems.

By now it was February 1946 but even in the aftermath of
war the world is a small place. On our first venture to the
'Crusader' we saw three Irish Guardsmen approaching. One
looked very familiar, a mate from childhood cellar days in
Bostock Street, John Lyons, or, as I knew him, Waller Owens.
Just to confuse matters that evening, among his army pals he
had acquired the nickname of 'Tiger'. We had a long chat on
the pavement and then went on for a celebratory drink. He
even arranged a lift back for us. Needless to say we agreed to
meet again but never did.

Back at the hospital that night I began to feel disastrously
ill. I knew it was not the drink; we were still not getting paid
and poverty had necessitated moderation. The next morning
the nurse as a matter of routine took my temperature and then
sped off to get Annie. As quick as lightning and without any

A and C Coy's Jeeps at the Battalion Rest Club, near Buckeburg, shortly after the war ended.

fuss, I was rushed back into isolation; something had gone very badly wrong with my wound. I was put in bed under the strictest orders to stay put until further notice. I was scarcely in a position to disobey, completely exhausted and sweating cobs. The rest of the week was a blur; I remember hearing a voice babbling away incoherently in the background. After a while it dawned on me that it was a Roman Catholic priest and I had enough religious nouse to realise I was getting the Last Rites. So this was it; my number was finally up. I genuinely did not care: I was tired and had had enough. Yet on regaining consciousness it turned out two days had elapsed since I had been prepared to meet my maker. It was still touch and go but a couple of mates from the general ward were allowed short visits to improve my failing spirits. I was very low and took it harder than most given my usual 'Here today, tomorrow we die' attitude to life. Dear Annie, no longer the tyrant of my first resurrection, spent hours trying to rally me with stories of getting ready to go home, to little effect. Temporarily I had given up: I could not see what there was to live for in my personal post-war reconstruction. Nevertheless my melancholic peace was then smashed by an overbearingly jolly nutcase who burst into my room like a younger version of Margaret Rutherford.

'Now, John,' she boomed with uncomfortable familiarity, 'how about a radio request, perhaps for your sweetheart or your mother? Have you a favourite song?'

She then went on to explain with gusto about the morale boosting qualities of 'Forces Favourites', a radio programme which, she emphasised, worked wonders, even for cases like me. The last remark was at worst ominous, at best tactless. In order to get rid of her and get back to the serious but peaceful business of dying, I painfully muttered that anything would do as I was not particularly musical.

Two days later, with great ceremony, the nursing staff brought the radio into my room in time for the much awaited programme. 'Margaret Rutherfords's propaganda had evidently had its desired effects upon the staff if not on me. Annie sat with me, beaming and uncharacteristically patting my hand. Then it started.

'I'm going on a sentimental journey ...'

I could not believe my ears! That the silly bitch had picked such lyrics for a man who had all but been told he was dying. I shouted out in anger; in later years I roared with laughter. Annie looked suitably annoyed and immediately switched it off as I dramatically screamed out how much I hated it. That was it! It was one of the major turning points in my life. I was beside myself with rage. I refused to die. I would not give the Forces Favourites organisation and that bloody song the

What was Bremen, from the top of Beck's brewery.

satisfaction. I amazed even the medical staff and eight days later I was back in the general ward with all my old mates planning more excursions to Lubeck *et al.* Perhaps the woman from the radio network had been right all along.

Life then settled down into regular outings to the 'Crusader' to break the monotony of recuperation. We hospital customers were, however, seriously short of hard cash, English BAF money, as we were still officially sick and not being paid. Eventually we came up with a scurrilous plan to improve our finances. Taffy acquired for us some cap badges from his mates in the military police and 'red covers' to put over our caps 'when on duty'. At this point the black market at the 'Crusader' was at its height. By the club entrance there was a path lined with four foot high privet hedges. One of these backed on to a local park where Germans would assemble to ply their trade. They were not, for the most part, decent respectable local people but free-loaders, parasites who had already fed on their own kind; our consciences had few qualms about upsetting their trade. They all came armed with briefcases full of watches and cheap jewellery which they had conned from more genuine people. Occasionally we would wait until a couple started trading with a group of eager squaddies. The latter were of course

The leading section of the Battalion passes through Bremen.

breaking every rule in the book. Then we would walk up on
them, red covers on our caps. Some mug would always spot
us and screech 'Police!' There would be a survival of the fittest
scatter and nine time out of ten one of the Gerries would drop
his case. The spoils of war were then ours, a lucrative form
of income. We sold anything of any worth far cheaper than
the real marketeers and gave the junk away to fellow squaddies.
The only thing we really worried about was our poor state of
health; neither of us were fit enough for either fight or flight.
If anyone had stood up to us we would have had it.

By now I had been in the Hamburg hospital for nearly a year.
My health was improving and I began to get homesick. I nagged
the staff about Blighty until they avoided me in the ward. Eventually I was informed that I was going to Travemunde, a
convalescent spot on the Baltic. Then my position would be
reappraised. Off I went for over four months of sheer, unadulterated luxury. The facilities were unbelievable, top class
hotels, a sort of German Riviera before the war, beautiful
beaches with whole sections reserved unashamedly for the recu-
perating British occupiers, superb NAAFI canteens, the best of
cuisine. We had everything a travel programme could think of,
motor boats, summer sports, horse riding, dancing, drinking and,
above all, sunbathing effortlessly in glorious weather. Arcadia
in northern Europe. Life was worth living again.

Again my spirits were boosted by a total surprise; one day
when I was doing my usual languid impersonation of a sun-
bather-would-be-playboy, a request came over the tannoy sys-
tem that I was to return to reception. Strolling back I saw a
couple of motor bikes, two three-ton trucks and a Humber
Snipe staff car, all occupied by drinking, smoking MPs. Past
misdemeanours niggled at the back of my brain. On entering
the foyer a chap jumped up and on me, arms banging the
delicate back. He smelt curiously familiar. When I finally
dragged him off, my face lit up. It was George, my brother.
A relative! Home! Football, Scouse, My Mam, Liverpool! I
visibly choked and spluttered.

It turned out that George, in the RASC, had been assigned to drive a brigadier in the smart Humber Snipe. The MPs were with him and they were returning to Blighty after service in Italy first overland and then via Cuxhaven. My mother had mentioned 94 BMH in a recent letter he had received and he had asked his CO if they could pay me a visit in Hamburg as they had a week to kill before sailing. The guy was all for it and had used his influence in Hamburg to find out about my 'posting' to Travemunde. The next few hours were full of news, nostalgia and alcohol. Once I had calmed down, George finally got to the point, 'How the bloody hell did you get in that state? You look as if you've been in one of them concentration camps!'

It came as a bit of a shock to me, a flicker of reality. There was I, thinking I looked great yet I had not clocked myself properly in the mirror. I had been over twelve stone just before my capture but now I weighed seven stone two and had actually put on several pounds. I had to confess some of the truth; George looked grim, but promised to keep it from my mother. He and his pals then managed to get a berth for the night and the celebrating continued until the early hours. Yet when he left the next day I was surprisingly down. I was now really homesick. I wanted to go home, start again, who knows, maybe even put on some weight. I immediately requested and was granted an appointment with the officer in charge of the hotel.

'Can you get me transferred back to 94 BMH please sir?' I implored.

'Why? You've only got ten days left here anyway.' He seemed friendly but a bit put out.

'You need to go back to the hospital before you can get home,' I babbled.

He nodded sympathetically and then with a paternalism rare in my army experience he persuaded me to stick to the arrangements and enjoy ten days more sunshine.

The days passed slowly despite the luxury. I was obsessed with home. Eventually I got back to the old ward at 94 BMH.

A good many of the chaps had left but the staff were out in full for a warm welcome home party. Annie beamed as Peter made a proficient speech in English about how much they had missed me. I was delighted. Annie then took me aside and said I was going home in a fortnight, on 4 September; until then she would have no able-bodied shirkers on her ward and had a million jobs to keep me occupied. She was true to her word and the two weeks flew by as I became an unofficial medical orderly.

As the time approached to leave I was given a thorough medical and spent several hours saying goodbye to an institution which had been home for too long. I toured the grounds many times, slowly, deliberately trying to make a mental record. I had a feeling I would never return; back in the real world I might not even want to. I finally had to say farewell to some of the finest people I have ever had the privilege to know: all the doctors made a point of visiting me and I thanked them profusely for their hard work and skill. Two Gun Annie, Peter and the nursing staff were more problematic. I could not find the words to express my heartfelt gratitude. In a series of clumsy gestures and hugs bordering on rough embarrassment I muttered emotionally, incoherently. Annie looked full, Peter smiling, clasped my hand repeatedly. The general sentiment was 'Good luck and God bless.'

Thus I left for the ship, driven in style in yet another Humber Snipe to Cuxhaven. On the quayside I bumped into the major who had been in charge of my case throughout my stay at 94 BMH and had actually performed all those tortuous operations. He was friendly but blunt, 'A word of advice, John. Take things very easy. Oh, enjoy yourself but don't overdo things. I don't mean to frighten you but unless you're sensible you won't be around this time next year.'

I thanked him for all his efforts, although his words had knocked me for six. I stalked up the gang plank minus some of the swagger I had had half an hour earlier. I waved to him from the deck and then went straight to my bunk and stayed there, wide awake all night until Hull. England at last! Disembarkation was a blur of red tape and uniforms. I was then whisked off by army ambulance to York Military Hospital for a day of examinations and documentation. Finally a new uniform, some pay and a railway warrant were issued. I had over five months leave due and jumped the first train to Liverpool. I agonized for it to go faster over every mile of track. Needless to say I dozed off and was waken roughly by a porter, 'Heh, pal, Lime Street.'

Music to my ears! I walked out of the station, sucking in the air, the accents, the cold hint of autumn in the dinge of a city centre. No tram or bus for me this time, I hailed a taxi and went straight to my Mam's. I was so excited I cannot recall paying the driver. I paused a second and then knocked. My youngest brother answered the door; he had been all but a toddler when I had left.

'Chris, Chris, it's me, John.' I spoke so quickly, so desperately that I gave him a fright.

'Mam! Mam! Mam! Come down! Mam!' He yelled as my mother appeared looking over a landing railing at the top of a narrow flight of stairs. I pushed him aside and rushed up and held her. God, she was grey! She sobbed her heart out. I thought she would never stop.

'Are yer all right? Are yer all right? Thank God, oh, thank God!' A large woman at the best of times, she heaved with emotion. Then normality returned.

'Do yer want a cup of tea?'

I smiled and nodded. Tea is a great leveller. As we sat in the kitchen, I was shocked at the deplorable flat she now called home. I had forgotten the reality of pre-war housing; I had seen better.

'How the bloody hell do you come to be living here?' I asked, angry at this slum above a burned-out shop.

'Eh, John, behave! It's been no bed of roses here in the last few years. We were bombed out and got a house in Bootle. The people had been evacuated but, fair enough, they came back when it was over and claimed their home back. Would to God we could have done the same but this is all we could get and we were lucky at that. Have yer forgotten the Blitz?'

I accepted the telling-off with good grace but made it my first resolution to get her rehoused immediately. I was hungry for action and felt bitter at her plight. I decided she had been pushed around because she was a widow, but now her Robin Hood was home. We spent a few hours talking, even gossiping. I listened to tales about relatives and neighbours I would have dodged before the war, but there was something refreshingly normal about trivia and tittle-tattle. Above all it kept her off my war. I then went out to get drunk. I was unsuccessful but luckily met a local councillor, Dave Cowley; I explained my mother's position but he was more interested in my war: George had not been as silent as I would have liked.

The next morning I washed and shaved and, tired of years of service, indulged my quest for respectability and borrowed one of my brother's suits. It was a bit big but would do for the housing department then down at Blackburn Chambers at the corner of Fontenoy and Dale Streets. Here there was a policeman on the door. Tempers evidently ran high in this public service. Inside there was quite a queue waiting for a turn at a huge counter behind which three housing officials were protected by three foot high gleaming brass railings. These three, two women and an officious looking forty year old man, seemed to just row with client after client. I suppose there was little they could do. Each in the queue approached the counter, had their argument and were then ushered out by the constable. There was an air of ritual, even farce. Then it was me. As quietly and as simply as possible I stated my mother's case. Then the male official absolutely shattered me.

'Well, what's yer complaint, pal? Yer mam should count herself lucky!'

'But she needs rehousing. The place stinks. I've got a kid brother.'

'Look you, we have men coming home from the war, blokes who've done their bit, not sit on their arse all day in the ale house in a posh suit. They're our top priority. If yer that bothered, why don't yer join up yerself. Yer look just about old enough.'

I felt my head explode. Bugger the health warning! I jumped over the railings like greased lightning and pinned the bastard on the floor.

'How dare you talk to me like that' I yelled almost pompously as the policeman dragged me off and two others arrived, arrested me and took me to Cheapside Bridewell.

'Empty your pockets, lad.' Said Dixon behind the desk. Out fell the army pay book. His attitude mellowed.

'When did you get home? This is new.'

'Yesterday.' I took a fit of coughing. The jump had done its worst and even I was scared.

'Get the fella some water, for Christ's sake,' the desk sergeant yelled.

'Look, you okay? We're going to have to keep you in a cell, see you all right but is there anyone we could contact?' With more presence of mind than usual I mentioned Dave Cowley. It impressed. I promised to behave myself if I could sit in the office. I could not face another cell. He agreed. An hour later my guardian angel arrived and gave them some version of my war record. He then said he would be back in a jiffy and soon returned with a piece of paper, a written, indeed sincere apology from the housing clerk who refused to press charges. The sergeant, accompanied by now by an inspector, came for a chat, shook my hand and said it had all been a terrible mistake. Off I went to 'Rigby's' for a pint with Dave, who promised to get my Mam rehoused, a promise which was speedily honoured.

As I staggered out of 'Rigby's' and headed back towards the city, taunting voices whispered inside my head, 'Peace in our time', 'Land fit for heroes', 'Twelve months to live.'

Yes, I thought, and you pass this way only once; so, here goes. The rest, as they say, is history.

Appendix

Extract from the Royal Norfolk Regimental Records:

Roll of Honour
(Those killed in battle)

271320	Lieut	G. M. C. Toft	June 1944
231603	Lieut	J. F. Campbell	6
196438	Lieut	W. M. Sharp	7
273652	Lieut	J. F. J. Williams	
62355	Major	F. Fitch, MC	12
307452	2/Lieut	J. E. D. Treherne	19
			(Died of wounds)
253653	Lieut	J. D. Drew	24 July 1944
52520	Capt	R. S. Elford	9 August 1944
327313	2/Lieut	J. R. Williams	16 October 1944
109406	Major	D. W. Smith, MC	27 February 1945
228159	Lieut	L. Dawson	1 March 1944
324318	Lieut	N. W. Rowe	
336804	Lieut	G. A. Smith, MM	
315734	Lieut	T. M. Rourke, MC	
CDN 171	Lieut	J. A. Laurie, MC	16 April 1945

331194	2/Lieut	H. M. Fisher	10 March 1945 (Accidental death)
5771384	Bdm	Dinwwodie, H.	6 June 1944
5778737	Cpl	Cobon, J.	
5956830	Pte	Lambert, A.	
5772625	Pte	Woolf, A.	
6437757	L/Sgt	Hollox, G.	
5783204	Pte	Attew, R.	
7953941	Pte	Baldwin, G	
5777744	Pte	Gillingwater, R.	
5771706	L/Cpl	Thompson, W.	
14413180	Pte	Cook, R.	
5777781	Pte	Hurrell, H.	
3602771	Pte	Barker, A.	
14331016	Pte	Longdon, H.	
5772388	Dmr.	Allen, J.	7
14410308	Pte	Mussett, J.	
6206710	Pte	Caudwell, J.	
5783324	Pte	Hales, G.	
5780086	Pte	Asseter, C.	
5784240	Pte	Taylor, H.	
91828	Capt.	M. R. Fearon	(Died as prisoner of war)
14618257	Cpl	Goerge, D.	
5888703	Pte	Noble, R.	
5772011	Pte	Symonds, S.	
14409748	Pte	Jarvis, H.	8
5771870	L/Sgt	Clark, F.	
5777527	Sgt	Purling, J.	11
6008890	Pte	Parker, J.	19
5775884	Pte	Scott, C.	27
5783748	L/Sgt	Walter, J.	13
402003	Pte	Glen, T.	4 July 1944
5769968	CSM	Gainsbury, J.	8
5776503	Pte	Morton, E.	
5890650	Pte	Toseland, P.	

5783355	Pte	Lincoln, R.	
14421971	Pte	Entwhistle, D.	
5779534	Cpl	Bowman, J.	
14674589	Pte	Davis, G.	
14414298	Pte	Larker, E.	
14631813	L/Cpl	Johnson, R.	
5777035	Pte	Wallis, A.	
14528954	Pte	Ormston, J.	
14407623	Pte	Coyte, J.	
5771650	Pte	Last, S.	
14631614	Pte	Brown, D.	
5773076	Pte	Hall, D.	
5775833	Cpl	Wood, J.	
5773552	Cpl	Bird, S.	
5772125	Pte	Jermany, E.	
5773518	Pte	Bradshaw, C.	
5771832	Dmr.	Holroyd, L.	
5778769	Pte	Fox, L.	
5771993	Cpl	Wright, W.	
14402887	L/Cpl	Fisher, J.	
14414305	Pte	Stolworthy, J.	
14404510	L/Cpl	Manlow, A.	
14408104	Pte	Frankland, L.	9
14414921	Pte	Townsend, R.	
14543305	Pte	Haste, B.	
14643370	Pte	Allen, A.	
6021075	Pte	Weston, J.	10
1567875	Pte	Mason, J.	18
14407766	Pte	Francis, D.	19
812979	Pte	Banwell, J.	20
5784270	Cpl	Bruce, A.	21
5778672	Cpl	Barham, F.	
14406646	Pte	Coe, R.	
5778748	Pte	Dunham, S.	
6151074	Pte	Jones, E.	
5783410	Pte	Thrower, A.	

5679620	Pte	Budd, F.	23
6149807	Pte	Fuller, E.	
5770769	Pte	Ballard, E.	25
5771704	L/Cpl	Jones, A.	4 August 1944
14413259	Pte	Hunt, C.	
5771679	L/Sgt	Wilson, A.	
5772279	Cpl	Mortimer, H.	
5784588	Pte	Tibbs, A.	
5116132	Pte	Bakewell, G.	5
5779760	Pte	Carroll, P.	
5116236	Pte	Evans, D.	
5784403	Cpl	Farthing, R.	
14329172	Pte	Waters, G.	
5673005	Pte	Board, J.	6
5932595	Sgt	Bruce, R.	
5112085	Pte	Barnett, J.	
5772242	Pte	Bircham, G.	
5773460	Pte	Bryant, A.	
5769927	L/Cpl	Chambers, F.	
5116206	Pte	Carter, C.	
14552816	Pte	Harris, R.	
14657095	Pte	Humphries, H.	
14404339	Pte	Insley, E.	
14408216	Pte	Makin, H.	
14416483	Pte	Moles, J.	
5776762	Pte	Nicholls, A.	
5776555	Sgt	Rehbein, C.	
14626579	Pte	Tomlin, J.	
5771770	Cpl	Wilson, R.	
5771629	Pte	Welch, W.	
5771955	Pte	Woolnough, R.	
6016653	Pte	Wood, A.	
146543412	Pte	Howling, H.	
14701631	Pte	Jackson, W.	
14214867	Pte	Jenner, D.	
1139478	Pte	Fuller, J.	7

5769530	Pte	McGrath, J.	
14295516	L/Cpl	Hammond, D.	
14568779	L/Cpl	Wright, E.	
14674764	L/Cpl	Bond, H.	
345953	Pte	Chapman, F.	
14404530	Pte	Metcalfe, K.	
14423790	Pte	Roberts, B.	
5779734	Cpl	Whitton, A.	
5779898	Cpl	Bates, S., VC	8
14669766	Pte	Walker, J.	
6289203	L/Sgt	Hills, H.	
14425942	Pte	Uniwin, H.	9
5122102	Pte	Conlon, F.	20
6479255	Pte	Taylor, J.	23 September 1944
5384521	Sgt	Parry, W.	24
3866087	Pte	Mansley, J.	4 October 1944
1114489	Pte	Wallis, A.	
4865417	Pte	Bennett, S.	5
6895703	Pte	Morley, J.	6
5961339	Pte	Ormond, H.	13
14426657	Pte	Anger, B.	14
5773761	L/Sgt	Cook, S.	
14416057	Pte	Crofton, W.	
14712419	Pte	Gorbell, H.	
3861331	Pte	Grundy, G.	
14714650	Pte	Halls, A.	
14425068	Pte	Hort, E.	
3865475	Pte	Kenyon, C.	
14285239	L/Cpl	Stork, W.	
5776530	L/Cpl	Earl, G.	
10537522	Pte	Cromack, P.	15
5777273	Cpl	Reynolds, L.	
5783628	L/Cpl	Longthorne, V.	
14611137	Pte	Jordan, A.	
14601169	Pte	Tull, R.	
5776013	CSM	Brown, L.	16

1830152	Pte	Cleary, J.	
5118748	L/Cpl	Drake, A.	
14568802	Pte	Hensby, J.	
14669135	Pte	Johnson, E.	
5771243	Pte	Johnson, E.	
5784253	Pte	Mann, G.	16
577429	L/Cpl	Moore, W.	
6412505	Pte	Sommerford, W.	
6476782	Pte	Miller, W.	
S/822395	Cpl	Emmerson, G.	
14283861	Pte	Gower, E.	
5733686	Cpl	Cahill, J.	
14543121	Pte	Seymour, K.	
14427755	Pte	Barritt, R.	
14438239	Pte	Wilkinson, R.	
14404949	Pte	Goodwin, D.	
6028978	Pte	Blowing, A.	17
5680480	Pte	Cox, J.	
14643234	Pte	Chaplin, F.	
5683066	Pte	Bindon, L.	
14413483	Cpl	Parkinson, F.	
14624713	L/Cpl	Moore, C.	
5784370	Pte	Aldridge, L.	18
5771996	Sgt	Ringer, E.	5 November 1944
5771938	Pte	Ewbank, D.	10
5772292	Pte	Rowland, W.	14
11001893	Pte	Webster, W.	18
3857873	Cpl	Fawcett, T.	
1495977	L/Sgt	Pegg, J.	20
5772907	Pte	Murphy, E.	22
			(Accidental death)
14331063	Pte	Rumbles, R.	23
5784290	Pte	Thompson, R.	
11406491	Pte	Hall, P.	28
14730538	Pte	Burgess, R.	3 February 1945
			(Accidental death)

14676587	Pte	Addy, G.	1 March 1945
5784268	L/Cpl	Basey, E.	
14766138	Pte	Bowden, G.	
5771763	Pte	Cator, J.	
5778948	Cpl	Cubitt, E.	
6085959	Cpl	Ferminger, J.	
14580975	Pte	Howman, H.	
989686	Pte	Lincoln, J.	
14722537	Pte	McCormack, E.	
14418839	Pte	Parker, K.	
14559796	Pte	Raison, A.	
5955820	Pte	Ratcliffe, G.	
5436178	Pte	Sowle, W.	
14413256	Pte	Barrett, D.	
5882368	Cpl	Biggs, F.	
6024265	Pte	Cariello, P.	
5776000	Sgt	Cole, D.	
5783677	Cpl	Duffy, J.	
1692344	Pte	Gable, J.	
14411423	Pte	Lennard-French, W.	
14722067	Pte	Miles, H.	
14660311	Pte	Onion, H.	
5783500	Pte	Parry, F.	
14494154	Pte	Rant, H.	
14316826	Pte	Robinson, K.	
5768460	Sgt	Stimpson, T.	
14709999	Pte	Andrews, R.	
5116194	Pte	Brayne, R.	
1151069	Pte	Garvey, M.	
14230886	Cpl	Morris, H.	
14520010	Pte	Warren, A.	
6481728	Pte	Young, E.	
5105461	Pte	Beech, B.	
5784180	Pte	Ditton, J.	
14626128	Pte	Ladd, C.	
14422868	Pte	Pottle, L.	

3392914	Pte	Williams, D.	
5780184	Pte	Cason, A.	4
859413	L/Cpl	Dugdale, E.	13
1799277	Pte	Connolly, J.	22
1625632	Pte	Akeroyd, W.	4 April 1945
2141429	Cpl	Boggan, W.	
14416010	Pte	Cosham, W.	
14571787	Pte	Snook, E.	
5772760	Pte	Rowland, A.	
5773861	Pte	Wrayburn, A.	5
14828045	Pte	Crossley, K.	
6024082	Pte	Massey, A.	6
14825557	Pte	Scofield, R.	14
14817379	Pte	Barrow, G.	15
14819501	Pte	Netherclift, C.	
14250093	Pte	Chapman, H.	
5775073	L/Cpl	Barwick, G.	